M000238874

Glorious
FREEDOM

Blessings!
Percy Burns
Ps. 124.7

Glorious FREEDOM

HOW TO EXPERIENCE DELIVERANCE
THROUGH THE POWER & AUTHORITY OF JESUS

PERCY BURNS

© Copyright 2020—Percy Burns

All rights reserved. This book is protected by the copyright laws of the United States of America. This book may not be copied or reprinted for commercial gain or profit. The use of short quotations or occasional page copying for personal or group study is permitted and encouraged. Permission will be granted upon request. Unless otherwise identified, Scripture quotations are taken from the NEW AMERICAN STANDARD BIBLE®, Copyright © 1960, 1962, 1963, 1968, 1971, 1972, 1973, 1975, 1977, 1995 by The Lockman Foundation. Used by permission. Scripture quotations marked NIV are from THE HOLY BIBLE, NEW INTERNATIONAL VERSION®, NIV®, Copyright © 1973, 1978, 1984, 2011 by Biblica, Inc.® Used by permission. All rights reserved worldwide. Scripture marked NKJV is taken from the New King James Version®. Copyright © 1982 by Thomas Nelson. Used by permission. All rights reserved. All emphasis within Scripture quotations is the author's own.

DESTINY IMAGE® PUBLISHERS, INC.
PO Box 310, Shippensburg, PA 17257-0310
"Promoting Inspired Lives."

This book and all other Destiny Image and Destiny Image Fiction books are available at Christian bookstores and distributors worldwide.

Cover design by Eileen Rockwell
Interior design by Susan Ramundo

For more information on foreign distributors, call 717-532-3040.
Or reach us on the Internet: www.destinyimage.com

ISBN 13 TP: 978-0-7684-5238-9
ISBN 13 EBook: 978-0-7684-5239-6

For Worldwide Distribution, Printed in the U.S.A.
1 2 3 4 5 6 / 23 22 21 20

DEDICATION

I express a huge thanks to my wife, Sara Jo, who has sat with me in hundreds of one-on-one ministry situations. That I am married to one of the most amazing persons I have ever known is a blessing beyond description.

Not only has she lived the ministry that will be described in this book with me, but also her writing skills have been invaluable. The endless hours she has put into the manuscript that has become this book cannot be numbered.

When I consider her contributions to our four children, their mates, and to our fourteen grandchildren, all who are walking with the Lord, I say, "No man is so richly blessed." It is a joy to see two more generations serving our Lord Jesus, giving leadership where God has placed them.

ENDORSEMENTS

I'm pleased to write an endorsement for *Glorious Freedom* because of what I know of Percy and Sara Jo Burns. Their integrity and obedience in this area of ministry is the result of a sober calling that was a surprise to them as much as anyone. And for all these years they have not used the ministry of deliverance for any other purpose but to glorify the Lord Jesus Christ. I have recommended Percy to numerous people suffering from strange symptoms and the result has always been positive—and usually extraordinary.

Dr. Tim Laniak
Professor of Biblical Studies, Gordon-Conwell Theological Seminary
Founder, ShepherdLeader.com
Cofounder, BibleJourney

"The Spirit of the Sovereign Lord is on me, because the Lord has anointed me to proclaim good news to the poor. He has sent me to bind up the brokenhearted, to proclaim freedom for the captives and release from darkness for the prisoners" (Isaiah 61:1 NIV). Over two thousand years ago, Jesus announced the fulfillment of this passage in the synagogue at Nazareth. Percy Burns has followed in his Master's footsteps and demonstrated the vibrant reality of this ministry for the past forty years. The book you hold in your hands wasn't written by someone who simply studied truth. The author has lived these words and seen the glorious freedom available through Jesus Christ come into the lives of thousands and thousands of people from all walks of life: children, teenagers, adults, men, women, rich, poor, educated, illiterate, pastors, missionaries, business leaders, and laborers. I've personally witnessed the fruit of this ministry and believe it's time to share the message and methodology of God's power to deliver people from bondage. Read, believe, and receive!

Robert Whitlow
Bestselling author of *The List*

As a Christian counselor for almost four decades, I have fought many spiritual battles, both with my clients and personally, as I have helped heal hurting souls. Percy's excellent book on spiritual warfare is informative, as well as practical, in exploring this concept. It offers a strong biblical perspective that is a must-read for pastors, counselors, and Christian leaders. *Glorious Freedom* is most helpful for any who have found themselves attacked by the enemy. Most importantly, it points readers in the direction of the Savior who truly sets captives free.

Drs. Tom and Beverly Rogers
Author of *Soul Healing Love* and Focus on the Family broadcast speaker

Many Christians have little or no awareness of the reality and power of demonic oppression. As missionary physicians serving in Africa and Central America, how well we remember seeing patients who consulted with witch doctors, even furtively bringing them into the hospital ward at night. Spiritual warfare and deliverance are key in helping people who are in such bondage in any culture. This book offers vital information and the scriptural foundation needed to set people free. It is a treasure!

Drs. Shaw and Sharon Yount

In this book, *Glorious Freedom*, Pastor Burns draws on his years of pastoral ministry and speaks to his experiences in deliverance ministry with simplicity and clarity. He lays out a scriptural foundation and adds testimonial evidence for the freedom many have come to experience under his ministry. The book is a gentle and unique combination of practical direction, inspirational encouragement, and theological enlightenment, bringing us to the unavoidable conclusion that God is equally at work in the modern age as He was in the biblical age.

Eric Newman
Lawyer and University Professor

As one who also ministers in the area of spiritual warfare, I have met and developed a friendship with Percy Burns. He has graciously allowed me watch his ministry with people. Our friendship over the years has been a blessing to me. Thank you, Percy, for sharing in this book just a little of what you have gleaned over your many years as a spiritual warrior in the kingdom of God.

David W. Appleby, MDiv, MA, PhD, PhD
Former University Professor
Author, *It's Only a Demon*

There is much discussion today on the rediscovery of spiritual gifts. I am grateful that, while deliverance and discernment of spirits is newer to some, Percy Burns has spent much of his life ministering to people struggling in areas of bondage. His new book shows deep commitment as a reformed pastor to take Scriptures, first as our guide, along with his personal stories and interactions in these areas that allow us to rediscover the freedom that Jesus came to bring and authority we have in the area of deliverance and the demonic.

Xan Hood
Author, *Sweat, Blood, and Tears: What God Uses to Make a Man*

CONTENTS

Preface   13

Introduction   17

Chapter One   The Launching Pad   23

Chapter Two   Recognizing a Demonic Problem   33

Chapter Three   How Demons Gain Access   41

Chapter Four   Step-by-Step Guide to Ministering Deliverance   55

Chapter Five   Ministering Deliverance to Children   73

Chapter Six   Recognizing the Power and Authority of Jesus   97

Chapter Seven   Personal Testimonies of Freedom   111

Chapter Eight   Questions You May Have   151

Chapter Nine   Called to Minister Deliverance?   163

Chapter Ten   A Journey through the Scriptures   179

Chapter Eleven   From My Bookshelves: Insights from Trusted Sources   217

Epilogue   235

About the Author   237

PREFACE

Spiritual warfare? Deliverance? Demons? These were all unfamiliar and almost unspoken words to me when I entered the ministry as a young man more than four decades ago. But over the years of being a mainline denominational pastor, I have encountered situation after situation that defied a seemingly normal pastoral approach. Individuals walked into my office with spiritual bondages from which they could not break free. Some brought their children and teens who were cruelly being tormented by an unexplained darkness. Families were desperately searching for answers and help that I did not have.

What was I missing?

In seminary I had been well instructed in many areas: biblical knowledge, exegesis of Scripture, study of the Greek and Hebrew languages, church history, pastoral counseling, etc. But no one touched upon the subject of spiritual warfare, the demonic, or deliverance, nor how that might be applied in ministry today.

The answer came as I became aware over a period of time and a series of events that we are engaged in a spiritual battle with the *"accuser of the brethren"* (Revelation 12:10) and that we have been given authority over that enemy by the Lord Jesus Himself. This is the story of my journey. But it doesn't stop there. I want you to learn how to be set free from spiritual bondages and how to minister freedom within your own family and to any others whom the Lord might bring to you.

I will share with you situations we encountered over the years in our own family and in the lives of those who came seeking help, which required a spiritual warfare approach to achieve results. I share these stories because I want hope to begin rising up in your heart. If victory over darkness has been illusive for you, I want faith to ignite as you read these powerful encounters of the Spirit of God setting people free.

I will teach you how you, too, can walk in the power and authority given you by Jesus Christ to be set free from demonic bondages and how to set others free. *Glorious Freedom* is for all who desire to recognize demonic strongholds in your own life or in your children's lives, how to deal with those bondages, and how to protect yourself and your family from the strategies of our common enemy Satan.

I have also included a chapter on the corporate ministry of deliverance, which gives spiritual and practical insights I have gained during forty-seven years of ministering deliverance within the church. This section will help equip those who feel that the ministry of deliverance may be one of God's callings on your life.

For now, we will look at the big picture to see how all of this spiritual warfare against darkness began. While there are different opinions and different streams of thought about the beginning of evil, much of Christianity accepts the following as the record of how it began.

THE BIG PICTURE

Before the creation of humankind, God created a host of perfect beings. Some of these beings we call angels. The word *angel* in the original language of the Bible means *messenger.* These messengers did the bidding of God. Leaders of these angels were called archangels.

Lucifer was one of those archangels. He led a revolt against God, and a host of angels and other created beings joined in this rebellion. Apparently, jealousy and the desire to rule in the place of God were at the core of this uprising. Lucifer and those who followed him in rebellion were defeated. They lost their place of leadership in God's universe and were driven from their places of authority and service. This accepted doctrine is gleaned from various parts of Scripture, especially in the Old Testament, and compiled to produce this information.

The original failure of these opponents did not end the warfare. The target of this rebellion against God became God's creation. The apex of His creation was their special target—the human race. The evil one deceived the original humans and led them into sin. From that time until today we are born with a sinful nature. The word *sin* in the original biblical language means *missing the mark*. That describes the condition of all of us. The very good news is that if we embrace Jesus Christ as Lord and Savior, the power of sin is broken in our lives. The sobering news, for those of us who have made this decision, is that we are still targets of the forces of darkness.

Lucifer became known by several names in Scripture. He is best known by two names, Satan and the devil. In his role as the leader of evil, he has an uncountable host of beings that do his bidding. Since the creation of humankind, Satan and his host have attacked God by attacking that which is loved most by God—humankind. We are the part of His creation made in His own image to have perfect fellowship with God Himself.

To rescue His creation, God gave His laws to His chosen people. He gave them the tabernacle and later the temple as places where sacrifice for sin could be made. He sent prophets to declare His holy will to the people and to call them away from idolatry to righteousness. Scribes recorded great acts of God for the generations that followed. But this was not enough.

Finally, God sent the very best He had to send. He sent His only Son, the Lord Jesus Christ, into our world to make it possible for humankind to honor Him while on earth and to spend eternity with Him, the Creator of this universe. The alternative was to spend eternity with the god of this world, Satan. Jesus Christ provided the way of salvation by His perfect life, by His intense suffering on the cross leading to death, by His glorious bodily resurrection, and His ascension into heaven. By faith in Christ and His accomplished work, humankind is given the only way to have fellowship with God and to spend eternity with Him. Because of the blood that was shed at the cross, Jesus made it possible for us, as believers in Him, to be victorious over Satan and his host.

Satan continues his war and his deception. But he is ultimately a defeated foe. The church has attempted to apply much of the wealth of truth of who Christ is to her people. But most church leadership has not been adequately equipped in understanding, administering, and teaching spiritual warfare. Consequently, Satan and his hosts have too often caused calamity in the lives of earnest people trying to follow the Lord.

As you read and experience God in this book, I encourage you to approach the subject prayerfully. You will learn about beings that are much more clever than you, and you will learn of the power and authority you, as a believer, have been given over them by the Lord Jesus. You will learn how to walk in that authority and break spiritual bondages under which so many are laboring. You will learn how to pray and minister to your family and to any others the Lord may send your way.

My hope and prayer is that *Glorious Freedom* will help awaken a fresh awareness of the subject of deliverance, or the casting out of demons, and its relevance for the Christian believer and our families in the twenty-first century. I want to dispel the fear and stigma and misunderstanding that has developed around this ministry. It is one of God's gracious gifts to the church. You may not agree with every word or every conclusion I have made, but I do hope you will give me a fair hearing and will ask the Holy Spirit to lead you into all truth.

DEFINITIONS

Definitions of terms used in this book:

- Demons (also called unclean spirits, evil spirits)—part of Satan's host

- Deliverance—the process of casting out demons

- Spiritual warfare—our efforts to resist and defeat Satan and his host, especially casting out spirits

INTRODUCTION

As we begin our journey looking at spiritual warfare, especially the deliverance aspect of it, I would like to share a story with you concerning someone who came to me desperate for help. This account is written in his own words:

I had heard about it before—and what I thought about it wasn't good. I am talking about deliverance. My mind went to some demon-possessed person, foaming at the mouth, pale in appearance, in a room with a man dressed in full religious robes and multiple cross necklaces! Not a comforting scene to say the least!

But…I was desperate! I was at the end of myself. Years of sexual addiction had created a stronghold over me. I had used up all the "chances" in my marriage. My latest and last mistake was it—the proverbial "final straw."

So when I met with Chuck, and he said, "I know a guy who can help you," I was quick to respond, "Yes, I will meet him." Chuck told me I had done all I could in terms of my treatment except for one thing. He was right. Despite years of counseling (individual, couple, and group), countless 12-step meetings, outpatient rehab, and ultimately inpatient rehab, I still was not well. My mind wasn't right. I didn't know it at that time, but I needed deliverance.

Chuck was very vague about "this man" who could help me and even more vague about the process. I didn't really ask any more questions, and he didn't offer any more information. He told me he would reach out to him and see if we could meet in the next day or so. He tried to reassure me by saying, "Don't worry, he does this type of ministry all the time." I am sure he saw the fear on my face and felt the pain of my situation as the tears came down my face. I had been kicked out of my house for what I thought was the last time.

We parted, and I spent the next several hours driving aimlessly around the city to numerous hotels, only to leave in fear and not check in. Finally, in pure exhaustion, I checked into a Holiday Inn, telling the clerk that I didn't know how long I would be staying. Later that night, I received a call from Chuck. He had spoken with the man and had lined up a meeting for the next evening! Chuck seemed very hopeful and excited that we could meet so quickly. At this point, I was desperate and willing to do anything to get free.

We met the next evening at the local YMCA, and he drove me to the man's house. Although I had never been there before, I immediately felt at home when we drove up. It felt safe, and I had peace as we walked down the side-walk to the home. We were warmly greeted at the front door by "the man" who now had a face and a name, Percy Burns. He brought us into his office; we all sat down, and he began to explain what he was going to do. He made me feel at ease and eliminated any fears I had. All my previous misconceptions about deliverance seemed to fade away as he began to minister to me.

He ministered for hours that first night and again the following night. Sitting here writing this several years later, I still cannot fully grasp or explain what happened those two nights. Percy didn't know my story, my specifics, my trauma, my pain, but yet the Holy Spirit revealed things to him and allowed him to minister powerfully to my soul—to the deepest areas of my heart! I am sure of this: I felt a burden, a weight (I would now call it a bondage) come off me. I felt lighter, and I felt freer. I knew I had my mind back! I also experienced physical warmth, an almost electrical-like sensation, throughout my body. This unusual feeling lasted for weeks! I would later come to understand this as the Baptism of Fire or the Holy Spirit.

However, the most impactful thing for me was that I felt the love of my eternal Father—a deep, soul-changing, accepting love. As I think back, that was the first time in my life that I had encountered His love for me in such a real, tangible way. I was filled with a sense of awe and love for God. I had tasted His goodness, and it was like nothing I could have imagined!

I left Percy's house forever changed, forever different. My gratefulness to his ministry cannot be expressed in words! My life since has been filled with the Lord's presence. His undeniable love, mercy, and grace has become the foundation of my witness to other men who are in my former situation, desperate and at the end of themselves. I can tell them there is hope! I am a living testimony to it!

—A man set free from sexual addiction

HIS WIFE'S PERSPECTIVE

I had lost all hope! My husband and I had done everything humanly possible to restore his mind, to restore my broken heart, and to restore our marriage. He would stand in church with his hands raised and tears falling from his eyes. I knew he was not winning the battle that raged within him. I knew he was asking God to take him. I could see the internal fight of my husband, trying in his own strength to be the man God was calling him to be. But he was not winning.

I could no longer handle the trauma I felt due to the betrayal of my husband to the covenant we had made to honor each other. I remember clear as day, with nothing left in me, lying on the sofa, praising God for who I knew He was. With tears streaming down my face and feeling so hopeless, I fully surrendered myself to the Lord and handed my husband over to Him. "I can no longer do this anymore," I sobbed to the Lord. It was the "I'm-completely-at-the-end-of-myself" moment. I felt as though I had just laid my husband at the feet of Jesus and walked away. It was heart-wrenching.

Earlier I had gone to a prayer group I regularly attend. My beautiful sisters had prayed over me, filling me with their faith and hope. One of them handed me a book on the subject of deliverance, and with it she gave me a man's name (Percy Burns) and his phone number. That afternoon I read the book and called the number, leaving a message that I wanted to make an appointment for my husband. (Yes, I would still do anything to help him.)

Later that evening, Percy returned my call. I told him that I would like to make an appointment and told him my husband's name. He repeated his name back to me to make sure he had heard me correctly and then proceeded to tell me that my husband had just left his home! I was dumbfounded! Percy began telling me that my husband was a godly man, that he was free and would be ready to come home. It was all such a blur. I still don't fully remember the extent of that conversation.

When I next saw my husband, I could just tell by his eyes and his demeanor that a drastic change had occurred within him. He had a Holy Spirit twinkle and a joy that I had never seen! He reminded me of David dancing in the streets while his wife scoffed down at him. (I hate admitting that now, but I rather felt like that back then because he was so full of joy.)

My husband, honestly, is a completely different man. He has been made new! I struggled for a while, adjusting to this new man and wondering what on earth had gone on. He was so different, so wonderfully different! Freedom, joy, love, peace, patience, self-control, overflowing, on fire, zealous! I came to realize that he had experienced Jesus' love for the first time and was so filled with God's presence that he has never been the same since!!!! Our loving Father is a miracle maker!

The redemption God has done in my personal life, our marriage, and our family is something I will never be able to forget for one minute. I thank

Him every day for what He has done. My desire is that every marriage suffering with this same circumstance will experience the healing touch of Jesus!!! He is alive!!! Alive, indeed!!!

—A most grateful wife

I share this story with you from the "get-go" for several reasons. First, I want you to begin to grasp hold of the reality of the demonic in our present-day world. Second, I want you to know that this book is filled with hope for anyone who has lost all hope. Answers are offered to those who have found no answers. And third, I want you to embrace the power and authority that Jesus has given to the body of Christ over demonic bondages. He indeed is our Deliverer!

Chapter One

THE LAUNCHING PAD

Put on the full armor of God, so that you will be able to stand firm against the schemes of the devil. For our struggle is not against flesh and blood, but against the rulers, against the powers, against the world forces of this darkness, against the spiritual forces of wickedness in the heavenly places. Therefore, take up the full armor of God, that you may be able to resist in the evil day, and having done everything, to stand firm (Ephesians 6:11-13).

MY PERSONAL INTRODUCTION TO DELIVERANCE

While serving a church that was a five-minute drive from the French Quarter in New Orleans, I found myself hungering for more of the presence of Jesus. I was a young pastor and had come to the conclusion that there had to be more to Christianity than I had experienced. This passion for Jesus led me to attend a three-day seminar taught by a former Cambridge professor.

On the second night of the seminar, this Christian intellect taught on spiritual warfare. Here I was, in a gathering of five hundred people, listening to a scholar speak on demonic possession! At no time in the four years I had spent in a Christian college or in the three years I had spent attending seminary, had anyone taught on this subject. And, if teaching on this subject for an hour was not enough, the speaker then gave an invitation at the conclusion of his presentation to come forward for ministry!

In my traditional Christian world, most pastors conclude their services with a benediction, and then everyone goes home. But here was a leader who was attempting to do what he had just taught. A ministry room had been set up and a ministry team was prepared to join him in ministering to those who sought help. As he gave the invitation, one-third of the people in attendance rose to their feet and went forward seeking ministry.

As I gazed at the crowd streaming forward around me, there were people of all ages and from all stations of life. Overwhelmed by the number of people who came forward, the teacher abandoned the small room idea and had the people gather in the front of the auditorium. He then began to minister to the large number who had responded. He cast demons out of those who were seeking freedom!

What was this? Up until that evening I had not even heard a teaching on spiritual warfare, much less had I ever seen someone casting out demons. I was shocked! Yet, knowing the Bible, I did not see the teacher doing anything contrary to Scripture. He would cast out spirits by calling them by the descriptive word or phrase that best described what the spirit did to the person it inhabited—such as a spirit of anger, a spirit of bitterness, a spirit of perversion, etc. It was done with more dignity than I might have expected.

In the services I led in my church, I would describe myself as a traditional pastor. I was so formal that I would not permit the church organist to play softly during the offering less it smack of emotionalism. Now, I was in a service unlike anything I had seen. After a long period of watching, I turned to my wife and said, "Well, I guess it's time to go."

SUDDENLY SOMETHING

As we were getting into our car, suddenly something started happening to me. I felt like my insides were churning; my heart was beating out of my chest. I mentioned my discomfort to my wife. She, being a most gracious lady, stepped out of character and said, "I don't know what is happening to you, but don't let it happen in the car. Go back inside." I think she thought I might throw up. Anyway, the look on my face startled her, and she was fearful she might not know what to do if "something" did happen. Again, you have to realize that neither of us had ever seen or heard what we had just witnessed during the past couple of hours.

Being a dutiful husband, I went back into the auditorium. One of the ministry teams began ministering one on one to me, commanding spirits to leave in the name of Jesus. In no way was the ministry loud or shocking. As I remember, I coughed a few times but did not throw up, much to my wife's relief. It was brief, to the point, and effective. In no way was I embarrassed. In the days that followed I honestly felt a change. I felt a freedom. Life was better.

Impressed with the ministry I had received and excited about the potential to help others who were in spiritual bondage, I began to extend this ministry to other people. I would tell people what the Bible had to say about spirits that invade us. Person after person declared they wanted the ministry. I was excited about the amazing gift of deliverance that God had given to the church, although most believers in North America and Europe have not been taught about this gift. Granted, I was a neophyte in praying for people to be set free of demonic torment, but good things happened as I stepped out in faith. God really showed up!

My wife and I began a meeting in our home where, among other things, we continued to learn about spiritual warfare. We would minister during those evening meetings to people who expressed a need for bondage to be removed. Even though we were novices, the Lord did significant things through us. Lives were set free.

Unlike today, there was little literature being written to help us learn this important ministry. I still remember an eighteen-page booklet by Derek Prince that gave instructions on the subject. I would learn from the booklet, which had a number of biblical references, and then would apply what I had learned to people who came seeking help.

DARK POWER

One memory I recall from that early era was a friend of mine asking me to minister to one of his friends. My friend Gillis, a French Cajun, explained that this acquaintance of his had supernatural powers. He related how she could lay a piece of paper on top of a shot glass and make a sort of windmill, the paper serving as the propeller. She then would command the propeller to turn right, and the paper would spin right. She would command the propeller to turn left, and it would turn in the opposite direction. So, not really knowing what to expect, I agreed to meet with this woman.

I still remember shaking her hand as she came to the front door and feeling a jolt through my body from the dark power that dwelt in her. Even though I was shocked by the demonic force inside her, I explained the ministry and proceeded to cast spirits out of her. She seemed to be helped by the ministry. Her friend was appreciative of the deliverance she had received. For me, I was sobered by the impact of the presence of darkness that flowed through her handshake.

At first, the new ministry was an adventure. It was a thrill to have authority over forces of darkness. Really, it was a secondhand authority. Christ had won that authority by His crucifixion and resurrection. I was simply applying the authority that He gives to His body to people in need. I had always enjoyed helping people in need. Soon though, it became work. There was so much need.

I continued faithfully fulfilling my pastoral duties in our church. Yet, people continued coming and desiring help because of bondage in their lives. I would estimate that deliverance, the name for this kind of ministry, took about 7 percent of my time. It was an important part of my ministry, but it did not overshadow my many other responsibilities in the several churches that I would serve in the years to come.

Over the years some of the members of the churches I served recoiled at the thought of their pastor ministering in spiritual warfare. But the majority of the people have been supportive, and many of them have desired ministry for themselves, or for their family members. I am grateful for their support over the years. As time has passed, I have seen many people come to accept the reality of this ministry. Still, it remains neglected in much of Christianity.

Upon retiring from the pastorate, I became a seminary chaplain. In retrospect, it would have been easy to leave behind the portion of my ministry that dealt with spiritual warfare. I could easily have felt that I had done my part and let others embrace this ministry of deliverance and continue the work. But I had seen too many lives changed and hope restored to have taken that easy route.

THE RIGHT TO WRITE?

What gives me the right to write this book? I have been doing this ministry for forty-seven years. I have ministered to several thousands of people one on one. I have taught seminars in churches. I have been asked to instruct ministry teams in churches how to cast out spirits. I have been invited to numerous home group Bible studies to teach and minister deliverance. Businessmen have asked me to come teach their "before work" Bible studies on this subject. I have spoken to seminary classes a number of times on the subject of deliverance. I have had opportunities to speak at seminary chapels on spiritual warfare.

I have ministered to all kinds of people. It has been my privilege to minister to countless pastors and their families and to missionaries and their families. I have ministered to scores of seminary students. I have ministered to individuals who have been referred by seven different professional counseling centers in our city. On occasion, I have done this ministry in the presence of several psychiatrists.

Some years ago I felt prompted by the Lord to focus on community leaders. To that end, God has sent business leaders, educational professionals, lawyers, physicians, etc., all seeking God's healing touch in the area of deliverance. I say none of this boastfully. I give all the praise to the Lord God for all He has accomplished in the lives of these precious people. I continue to be amazed at who comes seeking help! I do not advertise. I do not solicit. My calendar is full.

BUT WHY DID I NEED DELIVERANCE?

But why in the world had I needed deliverance? I just couldn't get the question out of my mind. I was not a troubled person or someone involved in the occult world. I was a Presbyterian pastor! I had joined the church at the age of ten and had sincerely embraced the Christian faith. By the grace of God, I did not get into much mischief growing up. I had a well-rounded youth, playing school sports and performing in school plays.

From an early age I became a student of the Bible, always seeking to know and serve the Lord. Again and again, in my studies of Scripture, I encountered words like *demons*, *evil spirits*, and *unclean spirits*. I remember distinctly as a teenager questioning my uncle, who was a pastor, about the meaning of a particular passage that dealt with the demonic. His only answer was to refer me to one of his volumes of Matthew Henry's commentaries and told me to read about it.

In many ways I had come from an accomplished and honorable family. On both my mother and father's sides there were very successful people. But there were also destructive activities. One of my great-grandfathers was a successful political figure and an officer in the church, but he was also a member of the Ku Klux Klan. One of my grandmothers was highly educated for her era. She and my grandfather entertained U.S. senators and governors in their home and were church members. Because of the early death of my grandfather, she came to live with us. Every morning she would tell her fortune at the breakfast table.

As I prayed and thought about my question, my conclusion was that I needed that ministry because of what had been passed down to me from my family line. There were destructive patterns in our family—alcoholism, anger, involvement in fortune telling, etc. I am convinced that some of these harmful patterns were caused by spiritual beings and opened me up to spiritual bondage. Part of what had been in generations before me had been passed down to me. I will cover this topic of generational bondages in more detail later in the book.

OUR HOMES SHOULD BE SPIRITUAL SAFE HAVENS

As I have mentioned before, the first church we served was a Presbyterian church in New Orleans, Louisiana. Living in this city was quite an adjustment for both of us. I was from a tiny town in Mississippi, and Sara Jo was from a small town in south Texas. New Orleans was a huge bustling city—and a city permeated with spiritual darkness.

When we first moved to New Orleans, an ordinance had just been passed prohibiting the practice of voodoo on the front lawn of City Hall. At that time New Orleans was considered the center of witchcraft for the nation. Crime was rampant, and racial tensions were high.

We lived near the French Quarter on one of the streets that actually borders the French Quarter. The church was right next door to our home. We would often hear gunshots in the middle of the night. Our church was broken into a number of times.

One day I was working out in the yard, and a woman asking if she might use our telephone approached me. (This was before cell phones.) She went on to explain that she had been in a car wreck, and she needed to call for help.

I want you to hear the rest of the story from Sara Jo's perspective:

> I was in the kitchen working, and I heard Percy walking up our back stairs. We lived on the top floor of a two-story house (the church offices were on the bottom floor). As I went to open the door for him, he said there was a woman who needed to use our phone because she was had been in a wreck.

> I invited her in. As soon as she stepped over the threshold of our home, she fell to the ground and began writhing on the floor. It was as though she had hit an invisible wall that knocked her down.

Percy and I stood there with our mouths open! There was a strange woman on our kitchen floor writhing like a snake! At that time in our lives, we knew very little about spiritual warfare. What I did know was that we had a two-month-old baby on the other side of that kitchen wall, and there was no way I was going to let this slithering woman get near him.

With everything within me and with the little knowledge I had, I began rebuking in the name of Jesus whatever it was possessing this woman and crying out for the Lord to protect our precious infant. As she slithered across our floor to the telephone, Percy joined me in confronting the demonic.

All of a sudden, she stopped slithering and crawled up on the sofa and began conversing with us as though nothing had happened. Percy said to her, "Ma'am, do you realize what you just did?" He began to talk with her about Jesus, but she didn't want to hear a word. She told us that she was a member of a cult just down the street from our home. She made her phone call, and went on her way.

That incident helped open our eyes once again to the reality of the demonic. This story didn't play out somewhere in a tribal village in a deep dark jungle halfway around the world; it occurred in our home! But what the Lord did reveal to me is that He is our protection. When that demon-possessed woman tried to enter our home, she encountered the powerful, yet invisible, presence of the Holy Spirit. She was knocked to the floor by Someone infinitely more powerful than the demon driving her.

The Lord was most gracious to us during our time in New Orleans. It was a teaching time, a time of preparation for what the Lord was calling us to in the years to come. It truly was a launching pad into a life of ministry that we could never have imagined.

QUESTIONS TO CONSIDER

1. Have you personally ever gone through a time when you hungered more for the felt presence of Jesus? How did that make you feel? What did you do about it?

2. Have you ever heard about the deliverance aspect of spiritual warfare?

3. Have you ever had any experiences where you wondered if the demonic was involved? Describe them.

PRAYER

Dear heavenly Father, as I begin this book, please be my Teacher. Speak to my heart by Your Holy Spirit. Lead me into Your truth concerning deliverance and spiritual warfare. In Jesus' name, amen.

Chapter Two

RECOGNIZING A DEMONIC PROBLEM

For though we walk in the flesh, we do not war according to the flesh, for the weapons of our warfare are not of the flesh, but divinely powerful for the destruction of fortresses (2 Corinthians 10:3-4).

Do you remember the man whose testimony appeared in the introduction of this book? The following account is the same story told from my perspective as the one ministering to this desperate man. There are several truths to learn from this situation.

A friend in ministry asked if he could bring an acquaintance of his over for me to minister deliverance to. The man had hit rock bottom in his marriage. The marriage was in crisis because of his serious sexual sin. The struggle he was facing was intensified by demonic bondage that had attacked him in this area of his life. I agreed to meet with this man.

The two men came over the next day. The three of us visited for a few minutes to break the ice, and then we got down to serious business. I went into detail about my experience of having spirits cast out of me even though, at the time, I had been in the pastorate for five years. We talked about what the Bible says about spiritual bondage.

Then I asked him if he wanted to receive ministry. Without hesitation he expressed his desire to proceed with the ministry. He wanted his family back. He was so sorry for all he had done, but he knew he needed supernatural help to overcome the unexplainable darkness of addiction that was driving him.

While you might think all of this would be a terrifying experience, it was just the opposite for this man. As I listened to what the Holy Spirit impressed upon my heart, I began commanding spiritual beings to come out of him. At some point in the intense ministry he began to cry out, "I feel God, I feel God!"

Truthfully, God moved so powerfully that there were moments I did not know what to say although I had been doing this ministry for a number of years! My thought was to be quiet and let the Holy Spirit have His mighty way. My wife, who was in another part of the house, said she sensed the holiness of the Lord's presence in such a profound way that she felt like she was on holy ground. She decided she should walk out of the house for the sake of the man's complete privacy with the Lord. She went outside and walked around the house praying for the ministry.

After observing the Spirit's sovereign work for some minutes, I began again to cast out spirits. This continued for some time. The other gentleman with us was supporting my ministry with affirmations and prayers. We encountered sexual spirits, a spirit of anger, a spirit of fear, a cheating spirit, a spirit that made him two different persons, an addicting spirit, and a spirit of self-hatred. You can see how a person could be wonderfully changed with such spirits driven from his life!

During the session I had several impressions from the Holy Spirit that I shared with the man receiving ministry. I sensed that God was calling him to be a leader in the faith realm and a leader in his profession. I also stated from the Holy Spirit that God was going to change him so mightily that his marriage would be saved and that he would be a better husband than he had ever been.

We planned a follow-up meeting. At that time we continued our ministry by making sure that nothing remained that we had commanded out in the first meeting. We helped him to understand what God had done in his life. We also recommended that he connect with a professional Christian counselor, find a mentor, and develop accountability partners. I placed books on spiritual warfare in his hands with the encouragement to read and understand how darkness works against the righteous.

We prayed that he would be powerfully filled with God's precious Holy Spirit. God did not disappoint. This gentleman is now giving leadership in several Christian groups; he is a leader in his profession; and his marriage is restored. He walks in freedom from the tormenting sexual addictions that had so bound him. With a thankful heart I marvel at what God did!

TRUTHS REVEALED

There are several truths that I want to point out in this man's story. *He knew he needed help.* As you remember from his testimony at the beginning of the book, he had sought out counselors, sexual addiction rehabilitation, etc. He recognized that what he had been involved in over the years was sinful and hurtful to his wife and children, but he was *driven* over and over to sexual sin.

What had started out as a sin problem had, over time, turned into a demonic problem. When we don't deal seriously with our fleshly nature and continue to yield over and over to our sin nature, we give an open door to the demons. This can be true of a number of spirits. A person who continually gets angry and doesn't deal with it as sin, can open the door for a controlling spirit of anger. It feels welcomed there. And so it goes.

Therefore, one way we can determine if the problem is demonic or not is a sense of being "driven." It doesn't excuse anyone's actions, but it does help pinpoint what steps need to be taken.

There can be other clues that point to a demonic problem. I will list just a few, but I am quick to say that this is not an exhaustive list. Anything that is excessive in nature or foreboding in emotion or defeating in living can indicate the activity of demons, especially if it is a defining lifestyle:

- Extremely fearful

- Consistently confused

- Defeated at every turn

- Foreboding sense of darkness

- Excessive meanness

- Overly controlling

- Addictive personality

- A "drivenness"

If you notice any of these clues or patterns in yourself or in your children, I strongly suggest you hear me out in this book. It is my hope this book will awaken you and equip you so that you do not become one more casualty to dark forces! The big temptation is to live life as if these personalities did not exist. Many people take this position and find themselves in serious bondage.

I write from decades of experience in confronting demonic forces. I have tried never to do anything that would go against God's revealed will as seen in Scripture. In those years of ministry I have made mistakes I am sure, but I have cast spirits out of thousands of people. Many have come back rejoicing with glowing reports of the tremendous transformation in their lives or in the lives of their family members. I do not present you with a theory but with that which I have lived for years. I stand amazed at what God has done. I give Him all the glory!

DO I NEED DISCIPLINE OR DELIVERANCE?

Do I need deliverance or just more discipline? This is a question I often hear. I learned decades ago that "deliverance does not take the place of discipline, and discipline does not take the place of deliverance." In other words, we need both.

In the testimony of the man delivered from sexual addictions, we see that he had tried to be disciplined in his own strength. That might have worked at first, but because of his continual, willful involvement in the sin over the years, his attempts at discipline later on had little effect. The demons found a way into this man's life through the willful sin. It took deliverance *and* disciplined obedience. I believe that is one reason why Jesus told the woman caught in adultery to *"go, and sin no more."*

I once ministered to a lady whose practice was to get up early in the morning and have an hour-long devotional. That was followed by an hour of exercise. Even though she lived a very disciplined life, she still sought and received deliverance. It was not a matter of "either, or" but both discipline and deliverance.

In contrast, a person may be dramatically set free by the ministry of deliverance but never attempts to bring Christian disciplines to bear in his or her life. Consequently, deliverance may not have the full effect in that person's life because he or she did not walk in discipline.

This ministry, like all ministries, depends on what you do with it. For the ministry of deliverance to have its full effect, a disciplined life must follow. The willful practice of a sinful life will allow demons that once came in to enter a person's life again.

For emphasis I repeat the quote, "Deliverance does not take the place of discipline, and discipline does not take the place of deliverance." It is important that we grasp this truth and make it part of the reality of our worldview. Some people have received deliverance and then made no changes in their lives. The long-term results were not nearly as good as they could have been had they walked in righteousness and self-control.

In contrast, some people are very disciplined, but they have bondages in their lives that wound those around them. Their lives also fall short of what they could have been with the freedom made possible by deliverance.

If you are like me, you love instant and dramatic changes in people. But in some people God works in different ways. After deliverance takes place, the Lord allows a person to learn to draw strength from Him and to exert personal discipline. Victory comes over a period of time rather than in a few ministry sessions. Either way He brings glory to Himself.

RECOGNIZING DESTRUCTIVE PATTERNS

One of the most important issues that will surface as you read this book is how to determine if the source of the problem you are facing is demonic. As you prayerfully examine the list of possible clues, be courageous and honest enough to recognize if any of these patterns are present in your life or your child's life. Are there any destructive patterns or sins that you cannot get victory over or resolve no matter how hard you try?

This could be an indication that the problem has become demonic in nature. It is time to suspect that the demonic is working against you.

If you are really brave, you could ask a trusted friend if he or she sees any destructive or driving tendencies in your life. The answer may be hard to hear, but be intentional in having an open ear. The Holy Spirit may be speaking through your friend.

I will amplify on the list of clues I gave earlier in the chapter just a bit more. One indicator of a destructive spirit's presence is bizarre thoughts that arise in your mind. Most of us have unwholesome and even dark thoughts that occasionally flit across our minds. I am not speaking of these kinds of thoughts. I speak of bizarre thoughts that are not you and have never been you. I suspect a demon to be behind this activity.

If you hear a voice speaking to you internally, encouraging you to do something you know is against God's will, it is a spirit. Sometimes, such "a voice" will try to get you to harm yourself or harm someone else. Or the "voice" tempts you to return to previous sins or addictions in your life. This "voice" may try to cause you to mistrust God or to convince you that God doesn't love you or cannot help you. Know that a demon has hacked into your thought process! The demon is trying to imitate the Holy Spirit promptings. Remember, the Holy Spirit never goes against God's Word, the Bible. The Holy Spirit *leads* us; demons *drive* us.

There may be times when you feel like another personality has taken over your inner being. For a brief period of time the "hacker" surfaces and spews out destructive words and actions. If something occasionally overshadows your personality and brings forth rage, wounding others, it might be a demonic force rearing its ugly head.

A frequent sense of confusion and or a struggle to learn and retain truth can be caused by demons. I realize that there are a number of "legitimate" factors that hinder our capacity to learn and to recall and to process what we have learned. But, if you are unusually indecisive and often don't think clearly, the reason could be the demonic. Scripture states that we have the mind of Christ. He wants us free from confusion.

Spirits often can cause depression. I am mindful, also, that there are medical and physical reasons that cause depression. But, if there is no medical or physical reason for the depression, its source could be demonic.

Hopefully, this will help you better identify whether the problem is demonic or not. Again, it is only a sampling of what you may be facing. I have said many times to people that I would rather "chase" something that is not there, than to ignore something that could be a demon in hiding.

Be encouraged! God is our Deliverer! He is your Deliverer; and if you have children, He is your children's Deliverer. You do not have to live the rest of your life with these forces of darkness. You can experience glorious freedom!

QUESTIONS TO CONSIDER

1. Can you explain how the man's sexual addiction problem had become demonic in nature?

2. In the list of clues that could point to a demonic problem which one surprised you the most? Why?

3. Is there anything in that list or in the amplification of the list that you see in yourself?

PRAYER

Dear Father, please search my heart. I don't want to be harboring anything of darkness. Lord, I look to You. Uncover what needs to be uncovered in my life. I trust You to bring freedom to me.

In Jesus' name, amen.

Chapter Three

HOW DEMONS GAIN ACCESS

But one whom you forgive anything, I forgive also; for indeed what I have forgiven…I did it for your sakes in the presence of Christ, so that no advantage would be taken of us by Satan; for we are not ignorant of his schemes (2 Corinthians 2:10-11).

We have seen in the previous chapter that one of the gateways demons gain access to us is through sin that is not dealt with, that is not repented of, and or is continually practiced.

There are other ways our sins can be an entry point for demons. I have designated what I call the *"Big Three"* sin roots of spiritual bondages. These are areas of activities we have participated in and have thus allowed spiritual forces to invade us. And, as the Scripture at the beginning of this chapter states, I do not want you to be *"ignorant of his* [Satan's] *schemes."*

The first is the use of **illegal drugs and opioid addiction.** If we trace the word *pharmacology* to its root usage, we discover that it comes from a word that means *to call down spirits by hallucinogenic drugs.* I recognize and appreciate medicine that is used by God to make us well and keep us well. I appreciate the professionals who make available those medicines for us. But I also know that when illegal drugs are used, demons often invade the one who uses those drugs. Even after the drug use is stopped, the demons that entered can still be present. This is one more important reason for our culture to stay away from illegal drug use!

The second of the big three reasons that demons invade many in our culture is because of *multiple sexual partners, or immorality* in general. Five times in Scripture the phrase *to become one* is used. You may have heard this wording used in wedding ceremonies. Four out of the five times it is used in Scripture it connotes a wondrous event. It is good that in the bond of marriage a male and a female become one physically, emotionally, and spiritually.

But the fifth time the phrase *two become one* is used, it is used with a negative connotation. It speaks of immorality and becoming one in spirit with the immoral person. We know this can have destructive psychological implications, and we know this can have destructive physical implications, such as sexually transmitted diseases. Also, there are spiritual ramifications because the immoral act is breaking one of the serious commandments of the Lord. In addition to all of these negative consequences, I have found that often demons are transmitted through sexual acts of immorality.

For example, on one occasion I was impressed by the Holy Spirit that a young lady I was ministering to had an occult spirit. She was an accomplished woman; she had a Master's degree and was a member of a fine evangelical church. As I commanded out the occult spirit, she stopped me and declared, "I have never had anything to do with the occult." I asked her if she had ever been intimate with someone who was involved in the occult. She admitted that she had lived with a man who was very deep in the occult. This confirmed what I had known for a long time— sexual acts outside of marriage allow demons to be transferred from one person to another. That is one more reason to walk in sexual morality! I continued to cast out the occult spirit.

That leads us to the *third major reason* that demons are able to invade people. It is because these people have been *involved in either the occult, New Age activities,*

superstitions, or in non-Christian religions. I have never ministered to anyone who was involved in one or more of these areas of darkness who did not need demons cast from them. Sometimes we carelessly participate in the events that have come from other parts of the world and carry with them the potential of spirits invading our lives. My counsel is to avoid spiritually dark events altogether.

Once, our family was invited to what we thought was a cultural event sponsored by acquaintances from an Asian nation. A chair was placed in the center of the room and a picture of a goddess was placed on the chair; people began to circle the chair dancing and worshiping the goddess. We quickly left! I am convinced that sometimes our exercise programs, our relaxation experiences, and our martial arts involvements connect us with non-Christian religions. I don't oppose any of these activities unless they have religious overtones that open us up to darkness.

As an example of even naïve interaction with the occult, I share with you the following letter I received several years ago from a missionary crying out for help for her son:

Hi Rev. Burns,

There is an avenue that I would like to explore with you that might be a possible source for the attacks on our son. I've been praying a lot about what is going on, and God brought this to my mind after I had a night terror attack of my own. (I have panic dreams a couple of times a month where I believe that I am dying, and I usually wake myself up screaming and wake up everyone else in the house.) We've been so focused on our time in Africa this never came to mind.

Right before I conceived my son I went on a mission trip to Slovakia with other ladies. While there we took a tour of a castle. This castle was located in a town known for its witchcraft. Everywhere you looked the shops had cultic signs and dark arts symbols. The castle, which was very old, was in the center of town and is still used as a central part of the town's demonic activities. We took a two-hour tour through this castle, and in every room they spoke of ghost tales and told of some kind of witchcraft practiced there. One room was a place where a witch, warlock, and some other kind of dark leader would get together every month and do séances and use the Ouija board to predict the future. Every Halloween, people of the town would pay to get locked inside the castle to have demons chase them all night. (These were not humans dressed as demons, but real demons.)

With all this said to paint the backdrop of this demonic place, there was a statue in the courtyard. I don't remember who it was, but it was some kind of ritualistic statue. I touched the statue. I couldn't tell you what possessed me to do that, but I did. In touching this, could I have opened the door to some kind of demonic attachment?

I went to Slovakia right before I conceived my son. He came out of the womb, not wanting me to hold or comfort him. My husband was the only one who could settle him down. He cried for two years, almost literally. You could tell that he had some kind of anxiety, because he cried every day in preschool, every day. I mean every day! Then we moved to Africa and his anxiety went through the roof. Right after we arrived in Africa, he said that he started seeing witches—the same thing that was so pronounced in Slovakia. Now, he is showing strong demonic manifestations.

During my son's manifestations, he often gets choked. During my dreams, I get choked and I die. One night I woke up screaming, "I'm dead, I'm dead." And my son often says that the demons are killing him and that he is dead. One night before I went to sleep, I felt something crawl up my legs and numb me, and I stopped it before it choked me. There just seems to be an eerie connection to what's going on with me and what's going on with my son. The only thing I can trace it back to is Slovakia, because I had panic dreams before Africa.

I have since renounced touching the statue and making myself more vulnerable to the occult. However, my son is still showing demonic manifestations. I know we have victory over this, but I would like to take the opportunity to see how we can empower our son to fight against this darkness. I want to renounce and close any doors that I may have opened in being stupidly naïve.

Thanks,

A Missionary

This precious woman brought her son to our home, and my wife and I prayed over them. This letter shows the reality of the demonic and the naivety of believers in casually interacting with the occult.

In our ministry time with them we came against spirits of the occult and in the name of Jesus broke their hold over this mother and son. Demons left, and the son was free of torment. As far as we know, they continue to experience victory and freedom.

SUPERSTITIONS

Even superstitions can border on the occult. Most parts of the world have regional superstitions that people observe. In the small town where I was raised, superstitions were prevalent. Friday the 13th was considered an unlucky day. If a black cat walked across your intended path, you did not continue your journey in that direction. Walking under a ladder brought bad luck, but if you threw salt over your shoulder, you "broke" the bad luck, and so it went. While all of this may appear silly, there are many people who participate in superstitions on a daily basis that can open them up to darkness.

When I was a youth, one of my uncles was mayor of our town and a member of a mainstream denominational church. He was known to "take warts off with a broom straw." That was nothing but superstition!

In the modern church's attempts to be broad-minded and to relate to the culture, it can sometimes dabble in New Age religions. We must realize that hurting people will grasp at anything that they perceive may relieve their physical or mental anguish. This can lead them into occult bondage.

In Deuteronomy 18:10-12 (NIV) we read these words:

> *Let no one be found among you who sacrifices their son or daughter in fire, who practices divination or sorcery, interprets omens, engages in witchcraft, or casts spells, or who is a medium or spiritist, or who consults with the dead. Anyone who does these things is detestable to the Lord....*

We have seen how our sins can allow demons to invade us. The use of illegal drugs and opioid addiction can be an entryway for the demonic, as well as involvement in the occult and sexual immorality. All of this involvement is an affront to the Lord, as well.

OTHER WAYS DEMONS GAIN ENTRANCE

There are three other ways that I have observed could be openings to demons. The **sins of others against us** can cause demons to invade us. Also, what I call *"word curses"* spoken over or against us can be an entryway. Sometimes, *traumatic events* of life open us up to evil. You may be thinking, *That isn't fair!* And you are absolutely right! It isn't fair, but *Satan never plays fair.* He will utilize every opportunity he can seize to take advantage of people made in God's image.

The sins of others against us can include domestic abuse, harsh treatment at work, sexual abuse, bullying, etc. Many times there is the feeling that what happened to them was their fault. As I have attempted to pastor many scores of people who have been horribly mistreated, I have observed that usually great psychological damage has been done, along with an invasion of demon activity.

Word curses, even those spoken in a careless manner, can open us to dark forces. Parents need especially to be aware that their words spoken to their children can have spiritually devastating effects. Things said such as, "You'll never amount to anything!" or, "You can't do anything right!" or even, "I wish you had never been born!" These curses need to be broken in the authority of Jesus and any demons that have gained entrance because of them need to be driven out.

We can even speak word curses over ourselves such as, "I'll never trust anyone again" or, "I'm so dumb," etc. Remember that Satan is a legalist, and he takes these words literally. These curses need to be broken in the authority of Jesus.

Traumatic events can also cause an invasion of darkness: a child wanders away from home, goes into the woods, and becomes lost; nobody was at fault. The parents were not negligent; the child was innocent in his wandering. But the child panics, and the spirit of fear comes into him at that point. Again, it is not fair.

Trying to help such people with good counseling techniques is advantageous, but it is not enough. They need deliverance from spirits that have unfairly invaded their lives. You may think their reaction to deliverance would be, "Oh, this is just too shocking for me to handle!" I have found just the opposite to be true; the ministry of deliverance gives people hope to be able to leave the unhappiness that has been a constant in their lives for so many years. If this ministry is expressed with calmness, kindness, and gentleness, a hurting person may leave the ministry setting encouraged and no longer hopeless.

I want to come back to the subject of generational sins, which I mentioned in the first chapter. There can be demons that are passed down through our family lines. Not only does Satan not play fair, he is also a legalist. Scripture speaks of affecting "the third or fourth generation"[1] spiritually. I have come to realize that, if we have a totally traditional family, we have thirty people influencing us in four generations.

Much of that influence was positive for me, but in most every family there are destructive activities that may allow darkness to invade the lives of the descendants. That was true in my case, and I believe that is why I needed the ministry of deliverance.

So, in four generations, thirty people have contributed many positive things to our development, as well as destructive patterns and weaknesses. Satan uses these patterns as his legal right to continue his destruction down through the generations! (We see patterns of divorce, suicide, alcoholism, immorality, etc. that seem to "run" in some families.) Remember, he does not play fair.

Often demons can be passed from one generation to another generation through these weaknesses. Sometimes, they skip a generation. So, grandfather could have had a destructive spirit; somehow father missed it, and it gets passed down to grandson. While there are psychological reasons for destructive patterns to pass from one generation to another, there are also spiritual reasons why this happens. During my years of ministry, I would estimate that two-fifths of all the demons I have cast out of people have come through their family lines. A person cannot choose the family into which he or she is born. But, a wise person can deal most seriously with bondages that have been inherited.

We have looked at a number of ways that spiritual bondages can get into us. Let me recap those for you. Again, I would say that this is not an exhaustive list:

- Continual involvement in sin

- Illegal drug use; opioid addiction

- Multiple sexual partners; immorality

- Involvement in the occult including horoscopes, Ouija board, fortune-telling, séances, New Age, etc.

- Sins of others against us

- Unforgiveness

- Word curses

- Traumatic events

- Generational curses

Different from some people who are used of God in the ministry of deliverance, I often recommend professional Christian counseling after deliverance. If you were in a combat setting and a roadside bomb exploded near you striking you with pieces of metal, as soon as it was possible a surgeon would remove the shrapnel. So, would you then joyfully leap up off of the operating table and be completely well? No, you would *begin* to get well. It would be a process that would take a period of time for you to be completely healed of the effects of the blast. So it is with the ministry of deliverance. A person experiences new freedom with the help of the Lord to rebuild his or her life!

Have you ever seen a double-barreled shotgun? It is a gun that breaks open and you place a shell in each of the two barrels of the shotgun. You can unload one of the barrels by taking the shell out and still have a loaded gun because there is a shell in the second barrel. In attempting to help hurting people, our tendency is to unload one barrel leaving the other barrel loaded. Someone may counsel the hurting one extensively and even bring other great ministries to bear such as teaching, discipleship, mentoring, etc. But if the demonic is not dealt with, it is still a loaded shotgun.

The opposite is also true. Demons can be driven from the hurting person, but they may also need Christian counseling, treatment for mental illness, accountability partners, or mentoring. Without these additional helps you still have a loaded shotgun. As an advocate for the ministry of deliverance, I do not want to diminish in any way the great importance of all the ministries the Lord Jesus has placed in His church for the welfare, happiness, and freedom of His people!

CAN CHRISTIANS BE POSSESSED BY DEMONS?

Over the years I have often been asked whether or not Christians can be possessed by demons. It is an excellent question, and one that should be of major relevance to the body of Christ. The word *possess* is what often troubles believers. My answer to this often-asked question is, "No, a Christian cannot be *possessed* by demons." Often, I hold up my Bible and say, "I possess this Bible; I own every page in it." A Christian belongs to God the Father through the accomplished work of Christ Jesus. Therefore, a Christian cannot be owned by demons. So, in answer to whether or not a Christian can be possessed by demons, the answer is "No." But, can Christians experience the presence of demons that need to be cast out? Yes!

Of the eighty-eight people who ministered deliverance in the New Testament, almost all of them ministered to the godliest people in the world at that time. We know that Philip ministered to the Samaritans, and Paul ministered to Gentiles. But as far as we know, the rest ministered to those whom God had chosen to be a special people who contributed greatly to our faith today.

The following illustration may be helpful in understanding this concept. We have no trouble believing that a rundown, dirty, deserted house could have a mouse living inside it. In fact, most likely there are many mice living inside that structure. Contrast that to a home that is wonderfully well maintained and has a loving family within its walls. Could that home have a mouse or even several mice living inside it? The answer, of course, is yes.

The first structure is most likely overrun with mice. We might even say it is possessed by mice. But the second structure, the lovely home, could be troubled by only a few mice. The wise homeowner would still desire to figure out how to get rid of the few troubling mice. We see that there is a difference between being overrun, or possessed, by something versus being troubled, or occupied, by something.

As we continue to discuss this question, I call your attention to other distressing invaders of our bodies. The most obvious is cancer. We ponder the pain, the distress, the loss of finances, and the loss of pleasure because of cancer cells. These cells are injurious to the physical bodies of many Christians. We also think of a tick bite that can penetrate the skin of a believer and cause serious illness. This malady has literally changed the personality of some believers and has left some semi-crippled.

Just as Christians struggle against disease that can invade us, so does a Christian struggle against the demonic that can also invade us. Jesus' death on the cross paid for us to be free of both. *"By His stripes we are healed"* (Isaiah 53:5 NKJV). Remember that the three main ministries of Jesus were to heal the sick, cast out demons, and to preach the kingdom of God. And He gave us, His followers, the authority to continue that war against sickness and the demonic wherever it is found.

I have not personally known of anyone who has consistently ministered deliverance who would say that a Christian couldn't be occupied by a demon. Some well-meaning, but misguided, people would declare that a Christian couldn't have a demon. If you hear this, you might ask that person how much deliverance he or she has ever ministered. Some of those self-appointed experts who say that Christians can't have a demon have never even seen the ministry of deliverance. If they saw it, their minds might be changed.

I understand why people struggle with this question. It is difficult for our minds to comprehend the reality of demons being present in Christians. To that end I have put together some "logical" bullet points that might help in sorting through this question. Finally, it comes down to a matter of trusting God's Word, the Bible, and acting upon it in faith.

- There is much in Scripture about spiritual warfare. If there is little we can do about it, why were these truths preserved for us?

- There is an inner witness of the Holy Spirit in endless believers that demons can be in a Christian.

- Many Christians testify about being greatly changed for the better after demons were cast out.

- Many godly people have personally seen a major change in Christians who have received deliverance.

- While there are many accounts of the reality of the demonic in Scripture, I would think it would clearly state believers do not need this ministry if it were not needed.

- When a person who was troubled with demons becomes a Christian, when do the demons leave? I have never heard a testimony that said demons left the moment I accepted Christ. If demons could stay in a person a day after salvation, why could they not stay a decade or longer?

- How can believers be "taken over" momentarily by another personality if there were no personalities in the believer?

- Many earnest believers know that there is darkness inside them that is troubling. They can't all be imagining the same thing.

- Many of the early church fathers wrote on this subject. I know of none who have said this couldn't happen to Christians.

- In places in the world where God is moving most powerfully, the ministry of deliverance is often practiced.

- Many Christian writers know and say Christians can have demons.

- Many believers are convinced there is something in their Christian family member that is more than sin or psychological problems.

- Multitudes of Christians are sincerely trying hard to walk with the Lord and they find themselves thwarted by demons within.

QUESTIONS TO CONSIDER

1. What are three main ways demons gain access?

2. Have you ever considered that Ouija Board games and horoscopes are spiritually dangerous and should be off-limits to the Christian?

3. In the list of ways spiritual bondages can have access to us, what surprised you the most?

PRAYER

Father, thank You that You are almighty! Show me where I may have allowed the enemy to gain access to me. Forgive me where I have dabbled in activities that are not honoring to You. Teach me how to deal with the demonic. In Jesus' name, amen.

ENDNOTE

1. See Exodus 20:5; 34:7; Numbers 14:18; Deuteronomy 5:9.

Chapter Four

STEP-BY-STEP GUIDE TO MINISTERING DELIVERANCE

These signs will accompany those who have believed: in My name they will cast out demons… (Mark 16:17).

But to each one is given the manifestation of the Spirit for the common good. For to one is given …the distinguishing of spirits (1 Corinthians 12:7-8,10).

We have explored how to recognize if a "problem" might be demonic in origin, and we have uncovered possible ways that dark forces can gain access to us. We will now look at the "how to" of getting rid of demonic forces. It is really not a complicated process. God is the One at work. We just have to step out in obedience, and He does "His thing"!

In Mark 16:17 we see that the first sign for those who believe is: *"They will cast out demons."* In First Corinthians 12, one of the gifts of the Spirit that is listed is the discernment of spirits. I interpret these two truths to mean the following:

First, casting out spirits occasionally is a general gift to the believer. Here I interpret *believer* to be a person committed to Christ as Lord and Savior. Second, there are some members of the body of Christ who are especially gifted and anointed by the Holy Spirit to minister in deliverance on a more regular basis.

Scripture is not very descriptive on the "how to" of deliverance. In Matthew 8:16 it says that Jesus *"cast out the spirits with a word."* In Matthew 8:32 Jesus *"said to them, 'Go!' And they came out...."* In other places, Scripture speaks of "rebuking" spirits or "commanding" them out. And out they came!

Scripture is also not extremely descriptive of what happened when the spirits were cast out. Often it just says, *"And Jesus cast them out."* There are other times when descriptions are given: the demons would cause the person to *"fall down before Him,"*[1] or *"they were coming out of them shouting with a loud voice."*[2] But in most of the references to demons being cast out it just states that they came out, or the person was healed. At times it was not a sensational process—but oh what freedom was achieved!

I want to share with you how I do deliverance. I find it to be very effective. Other gifted people may minister deliverance in a different way. The important truth to keep in mind is that as a Christian we have been given the authority to cast out demons by the Lord Jesus Himself.

1. I begin by sharing from my experience and from Scripture what deliverance is and why it is important.

2. I then pray over the ministry that is to take place, carefully giving Christ all the praise for what He will do. I pray protection over the person who is receiving ministry, over his or her family, over the one who is helping me, and his family. Then I lift up the same prayer for my family and myself.

3. Next, I break any destructive tendencies or demonic holds passed down through family lines—such as, but not limited to, alcoholism, immorality, occult involvement, suicide, divorce, etc. Sometimes the person has told me what destructive traits are in his or her family line; sometimes the Holy Spirit impresses me with

what it is; and sometimes I just break anything in general that has been passed down that is harmful.

4. I ask the person to forgive all who have wronged him or her in any way. (I usually have them do this silently in their heart.)

5. I ask the person to confess his or her sins, asking the Lord for forgiveness through the accomplished work of Christ (again, in silence).

6. Then, I ask the person to forgive him or herself.

7. Finally, I ask the person to confess and renounce any involvement with the occult, with New Age, with any non-Christian religion, or with superstitions.

8. After this preparation I move into commanding demons to come out by the authority of Christ and His blood. The Holy Spirit impresses me with things like anger, fear, rejection, etc. The person can also tell you what to cast out.

9. After ministry I always pray for an infilling of the Holy Spirit to fill up the vacuum created by the spirits leaving.

This is a brief outline that I will expound on and explain more in depth in this chapter.

THE SETTING

We think of the setting. The ideal setting would be a comfortable, private place where all who are participating have comfortable seats. Each person with a cell phone should silence the phone. I typically have a box of tissues in case the person receiving ministry should tear up. The person assisting in the ministry will have a notebook and a pen to take notes that will become the property of the one receiving ministry. Many times I also will have a notebook where I write down spirits that God is showing me so I can repeat the command to leave at the closing of the session.

Concerning personal preparation, I will have prayed about the ministry and often I will have asked other people to pray that the persons receiving ministry will be set free. I typically have a glass of water by me because there is a lot of speaking in the ministry.

There is a period of orientation before the ministry begins. I try to make the persons feel comfortable with light conversation. Those receiving ministry may be nervous, and the light conversation helps them relax and connect with those of us who will minister to them.

After a brief period of small talk, I shift gears and begin the session of ministry. Usually I go in one of two directions. I will begin to speak about how this was one of Jesus' major ministries and how He taught His followers to do this ministry. The other approach I take is to share my personal experience of receiving deliverance. Then I will talk about how people have come to me and the Lord has used me to minister to them. Often I will combine the two streams of thought.

During the session, I am intent on casting out spirits. I begin listening to what the Holy Spirit impresses to my mind. This is one way the gift of discernment of spirits operates. I then begin commanding out what the Holy Spirit shows me. There may be little or no observable reaction. Don't be concerned; things are happening in the spiritual realm! Sometimes impressions may be spoken by those who are ministering with me, as well as by the recipient of ministry himself. If the recipient asks a question, I will answer it. But our main focus is to cast out spirits. I try to prevent it from becoming a counseling session, although some counseling naturally takes place.

Be affirming to the person who is receiving the ministry of deliverance. Assure the person with words like, "It's not you I'm speaking to; it's the personality in you that is driving you to do destructive things." Often I say, "You're not like a leper with spots. This is normal for people I minister to." When I come against sexual spirits, I will inform them that 80 percent of the adults I minister to, both men and women, have sexual spirits.

I may continue, "It doesn't make you any less a sexual being to have the spirits cast out. The spirit misdirects your sexuality." I often use a quote from a book I read, "Fire in the fireplace on a cold winter night is a good thing. Fire in any other part of the house is not a good thing. So it is with sex. Sex in marriage is a good thing; sex in any other situation is not a good thing."

I usually tell the person to whom I am ministering that I also have received deliverance. I want them to know that I am ministering to them on level ground. I am not ministering down to them. When a session of deliverance is completed, I want the person receiving deliverance to leave feeling affirmed and loved.

When I end a ministry session, I typically pray that God will fill the person with His Holy Spirit. Just as nature abhors a vacuum, so in the spiritual world the same principle exists. In the natural world something will fill a vacuum—air, water, or dirt will rush in to fill the emptiness. So it is in the spiritual realm. We have created a vacuum. In the name of Jesus, spirits have been ordered out of a person. Therefore, there is more room for the Spirit of God to fill the person by filling these empty places that have been left. So I pray and ask the Lord to fill the person with His Holy Spirit.

I extend reassurance to the person(s) after the session. I offer hope and encouragement. I typically will place books on deliverance and or spiritual warfare in their hands so they can learn more of the subject. Most who come are active in their churches. If they are not, I encourage them to get actively involved in a good church. I encourage them to find a mentor and a couple of accountability/prayer partners to help them break the patterns in their lives formed by demons.

Typically, I offer a second and even a third session if they seem to need the extra ministry. Sometimes we make such an arrangement before they leave. If circumstances permit, I prefer there to be several days or a week before the next session. This allows people to begin to recognize what good things have happened to them. We put calendars together and plan our next meeting. Other times, I leave the responsibility up to them to see if they are serious about wanting more help.

Again and again people who have received deliverance say, "I feel lighter." A physician I ministered to recently has commented several times since the initial ministry, "I think more clearly." Most people leave a deliverance session with hope that they can negotiate life. Sometimes a person who was moving toward an emotional breakdown was stopped from going over the edge because of the freedom and hope they received from deliverance. I always give the Lord the full credit for what He accomplished in our session together.

I cannot remember anyone leaving a session of deliverance in despair. Consistently they seem encouraged. They are appreciative. Usually they know something good has happened, and they are encouraged as they face the future.

We think of the New Testament accounts of all those people who received deliverance. There were no churches. Probably few homes had what we would think of as a living room or an office. Yet this powerful ministry still happened. Try to find a private and quiet place where other people cannot hear what happens. But if that does not exist, use what you have. Remember, it is God's work, and He can work in whatever setting He chooses.

OPERATING IN THE GIFT OF DISCERNMENT

I ask myself, "If I were reading this book, what would I want to know?" Possibly I was influenced to ask this question on your behalf by a physician who sought ministry from my wife and me. He asked this same question. I have referenced my answer earlier in the book, but I will try to amplify it to some measure. One of the many unanswerable questions in Scripture would be, "What was happening inside Peter, James, John, and Paul as they ministered in the same dimension?" Of course, we don't know. What we do know is the Holy Spirit was guiding them and empowering them to do this work.

As I have stated before, different people minister deliverance in different ways. I would never say that my way is the best way or the only way. I receive impressions from the Lord. Rarely is it a voice speaking to me. It is more like a thought that comes into my mind. Through years of experience I am usually able to discern what is an impression from the Holy Spirit versus what may be my own thought or a thought put there by a force of darkness. It is not a picture, although God speaks to some people through pictures He puts in their minds. It is not even a really strong impression that many Christians on occasions have. It is just a thought that I clothe in words. It is an insight into what the evil spirit does to the person or through the person.

Sometimes this impression begins to form days before I meet in a scheduled appointment with the one who has called out for help. Sometimes the insights begin when I am breaking generational curses that have been passed through family lines. But most of the time the impressions begin as I step out in faith and call out spirits that the Holy Spirit gives in the moment.

Therefore, I don't need to know beforehand what the needs of the person are. As I enter into ministry, the Holy Spirit gives me impressions and thoughts showing me what I should call out. Endless are the times people say to me, "How could you have known!" I explain to them that it is due to impressions from the Holy Spirit.

I do not get loud or weird as I minister. I calmly sit there in the authority of our risen Lord and do what He has commanded us to do, which is, in part, to cast out spirits in His name. I make every effort that the person understand it is God at work—it is not me.

If you do not feel that you have the gift of discernment, ask the Lord for it. As you step out in the ministry of deliverance, you can ask the person what spirits are bothering him or her. As he relates to you their names—anger, depression, etc.—begin commanding those spirits out. As you do so, be very sensitive to the Holy Spirit. He may begin impressing on your mind other spirits to call out. If you make a mistake, don't worry. It is better to attempt to chase away something that is not there than to leave something there!

SPIRIT-LED INSIGHTS

The primary focus of the ones ministering deliverance is simply to call demons out of the person receiving ministry. In addition, God may also use this time to speak His insights, encouragements, and or prophetic words through the person ministering to the one receiving help. The individual keeping notes of the meeting writes down the insights.

These insights could come in the form of Scripture passages the Lord brings to mind or impressions from the Holy Spirit. These Spirit-led insights could be very valuable as God is speaking His mind to the one receiving ministry. I recently ministered to a lady who is in ministry and who is the adult child of missionaries. We cast spirits out of her that had come in through tragic events in her childhood and then through many years of betrayal by her husband. Not only did God do this great work for her, but He also spoke through the two of us ministering to her words of great encouragement concerning her future in Christian ministry.

Therefore, in the ministry setting several things happened: she was loved and respected by the two of us ministering to her; demons were driven from her; and encouraging insights about her important work for the Lord were spoken. I fully believe that what happened to her will impact her for years to come in her strategic work.

DEMONIC VOICES

Some people involved in the deliverance ministry report sensational encounters with demons on occasions. People have told me that they have seen demons in the midst of ministry. Something like that almost never happens to me. I believe it is possible for the sensational to be experienced by some people in this good work. Frankly, I'm happy without the sensational experiences. I prefer the non-sensational encounters!

What I have experienced is an impression of the demons speaking, although I have not heard the actual voice of the demon, as mentioned previously. Sometimes the demon speaks through the voice of the person receiving deliverance, and I have experienced that on occasions. But sometimes I perceive what the demon is saying without hearing a voice actually speaking. I've perceived demons saying things like, "You can't make me leave," or, "This person doesn't want me to leave." It is not uncommon for me to perceive brief statements such as these.

What I do with this information is as follows. I say to the person receiving deliverance, "I sense the demon saying, 'I won't leave,' but I say in the authority of Jesus Christ that it will leave." Your response may be, "That would freak someone out!" On the contrary, I have never had anyone "freaked out." A take-home observation is this lesson: If you, as a minister of deliverance, have confidence in the Lord, it is easier for the person receiving ministry to have confidence and faith in the Lord. Some of that confidence and faith can come with experience. Neither the person receiving ministry nor the persons ministering have to experience the dramatic for life-changing events to occur.

PHYSICAL MANIFESTATIONS

Most of the time when I minister deliverance there is little, if any, physical manifestation. Occasionally, there are tears. I often keep a box of tissues on the table in front of the person receiving deliverance. At other times there may be more visible manifestations caused by a spirit. Sometimes the spirit takes over the personality of its host and uncomfortable things happen.

When this occurs, it can be disconcerting for the person receiving deliverance as well as for the persons ministering deliverance. If this happens, you have three options:

• First, you can gently conclude the ministry and plan for another meeting in the near future.

- Second, you can stop commanding the spirit to leave and begin speaking comforting words to settle the person down. Usually in a few minutes the person receiving ministry will relax. Following this, you can resume your commands for the spirit to leave.

- The third option, and the one I opt for, is to press in and be victorious over the spirit that is causing the manifestation.

There are times when I take authority over a spirit that is causing a person to shake or to cry uncontrollably. I order it to cease troubling the person. I then continue to command it to come out and leave.

As I have stated, most of the ministry sessions I have led have not been very dramatic. I think this is God's grace because in our Western culture most people shy away from excessive displays of emotion. In Scripture, though, there were tremendous outbursts of emotions and physical manifestations. But in our "sophisticated" culture, it is my opinion that many would shy away from seeking help if outbursts were a regular occasion.

But, there are times when dramatic manifestations do happen. Sometimes, in totally unexpected moments, the spirits inside a person will drive that person to bizarre actions. I don't want you to be caught off-guard. This doesn't happen often, but it can happen.

Years ago a psychiatrist friend brought his next-door neighbor, a young man in his mid-thirties, to me for deliverance. I knew nothing about this man, other than he was a Sunday School teacher in a Baptist church. As I began to command spirits out of him, he went into a rage. He began to cry out, "I'll kill you! I'll kill you!" He was not expressing a personal hatred of me because we had just met. It was the spirit within him manifesting.

If that weren't bad enough, he grabbed hold of the left armrest of my brand-new office chair where he was sitting and with supernatural strength broke the thick, solid-wood arm off the chair. Then with his right hand he broke the right armrest off the other side of the chair. He continued to scream, "I'll kill you! I'll kill you!"

My reaction was one of fear, to say the least. But the armrest stayed in his lap, and I continued to command the spirits to leave him. All the while I was trying to have enough faith to believe the power of Christ would bind the spirit. The ministry continued, and he was delivered from a number of spirits, including a spirit of violence. All ended well—except for a broken chair. After that I was more alert when I would encounter a spirit of violence.

On another occasion I was ministering to lady I did not know, nor did she know me. So, again, her reactions were not personal. This woman receiving ministry was a registered nurse. The ministry was proceeding well. But at an intense moment, as I was commanding a certain spirit to leave this woman, she made her hand into a claw shape and swung at my eyes.

I dodged the claw, which her hand had become, and continued the ministry. For the remainder of the ministry time, all went well. There, for a moment, a different being had taken over her personality and tried to do bodily injury to me. I did stay alert to what else might happen, but thankfully the demon did not manifest itself again.

A number of times over the years of casting out demons, the following has also happened. When I gave commands for spirits to leave, some people have fallen from a sitting position onto the floor. Sometimes they would simply lie on the floor as I continued to cast out spirits from them.

Occasionally, a person lying on the floor would begin to slither across the floor like a snake. This has startled friends who were assisting me in ministry. But my response was to continue to command the spirits out of the person. I knew from these manifestations that I was getting a response from the spirits tormenting the person. What may surprise you is that when the ministry was completed, no one seemed embarrassed that he or she had slithered across the floor. I am not even sure that they were aware of what they had just done.

I share these experiences with you not to frighten you, but to make you aware that physical manifestations of the demon can happen on rare occasions. Remember that you are ministering in the power and authority of Jesus Christ.

SPIRITS OF SELF-HATRED

Satan is described in Scripture as a liar, a murderer, and an accuser of believers. The hosts of darkness that follow him take on the same nature. Countless times in the ministry of deliverance I have encountered a spirit of self-hatred, a spirit of self-destruction, or a spirit of suicide. Sometimes all three of these spirits are in a person.

To understand that there are demons whose purpose is to try to make us take our own lives will explain, in part, why there are so many suicides in our culture. As I have come against one or more of the spirits just described, the person receiving ministry would confirm that suicide was indeed a problem that he or she had greatly struggled against. And many are the times these people would recount stories of relatives who took their own lives. As I look back over forty-seven years of ministering deliverance, I know of only one person who took his life after receiving this ministry.

If this ministry is accurately applied to people driven toward taking their own lives, I am totally convinced that many lives could be saved and made useful for the kingdom of God. Devoid of these destructive and lying spirits, the number of people taking their own lives would be greatly decreased. Christ is the life giver; the hosts of darkness are life takers.

MINISTERING OVER THE PHONE

I serve on the board of directors of a significant ministry that has headquarters around the world. The U.S. office is unique in that several of its staff people minister deliverance over the telephone. You may be wondering if this is even possible. I certainly believe the best arrangement is to be in the room with the person who is receiving ministry. But, the several people who are involved in praying deliverance over the telephone to persons who call in are having considerable success.

While this is not something I do very often, on occasion I have ministered over the telephone with God-honoring results. In one situation, the person was so transformed that the event was written up in a local newspaper. While I have only ministered a few times in decades over the phone, I'm convinced it has value.

Paul the apostle wrote prayers in letters, and those prayers were read weeks or even months later. It is as though those prayers went through time and space. Those of us who are serious about the Word of God have been touched by Paul's prayers that he wrote nearly two millennia ago. Therefore, I believe prayers of deliverance can be prayed over the telephone and be effective.

WHERE DO DEMONS GO?

An eighteen-year-old young woman once asked me an unanswerable question. She was sitting in a deliverance session and saw this ministry for the first time. She asked, "Where do demons go after they are cast out?" There are different theories to answer this question. Some people who minister in deliverance "cast them into the pit." I have heard one person give the command, "Go to the feet of Jesus."

My answer is that we don't really know where the demons go. It is my conviction that I have the authority in Christ to protect an area with His authority. If I am on the grounds of a church ministering deliverance to someone, my command is, "Don't touch anyone on these grounds." If a person has come to my home office, I give the command, "Don't touch anyone on this street." I often will say, "Don't ever enter this person again." Other times I will say, "Go far, far away." In a biblical account of casting out demons, Jesus commanded, "Don't enter this person again." Seeing Jesus ordering a spirit not to enter the person again gives me authority to make the same command.

One of the concerns of many who receive deliverance is the possibility that the spirits might come back. Jesus speaks of seven spirits returning where one spirit had been cast out. This frightens people. It sometimes keeps people from seeking a much-needed deliverance. My consistent answer is our protection comes by not engaging in the sins through which the demons had originally gained entrance. If a lying spirit has been cast out of someone, yet that person purposefully continues to lie, the lying spirit may well come back into the person. Our protection is to be obedient to the commands of God given in Scripture.

DEMONS CAN HARASS US BUT NOT BE IN US

Some forces of darkness are not in us to be cast out or located in some physical place to be driven away—rather, they come against us from without, putting temptations and tormenting thoughts into our minds. Their purpose is to cause us to suffer defeat as we seek to walk with the Lord each day.

How do we oppose the opposer? We drive him away from ourselves! In Revelation 12:11 (NKJV) we read, *"They overcame him by the blood of the Lamb and by the word of their testimony."* How did they overcome the accuser? They overcame him by the blood of the Lamb and by the word of their testimony.

When we feel an oppressive spirit opposing us, we can begin to speak out loud or to ourselves of what the blood of the Lamb does for us. "By the blood of the Lamb I am freed from my sins. The blood of Jesus Christ washes me clean. The blood Jesus shed on the cross is powerful against you." Do you remember the words of the old hymn, "There is power in the blood"? That blood overpowers our accuser.

The words of our testimony are powerful, too. We can say, "Jesus is my Savior; I belong to Him. Jesus is the Lamb of God. He is my Redeemer and Deliverer…." We testify to darkness who the Lord Jesus is to us. Darkness has to flee. It cannot stand against so powerful a testimony.

Another way demons can attack us from without is through other people. Most of us have seen a second personality take over a person during a contentious and intense encounter. Often, that is a demon operating in that person.

If you are in a conversation with someone and rage arises in that person for no reason, you may be encountering a spirit. In your heart you can command the spirit to be muzzled.

Jesus commanded the storm on the Sea of Galilee to be muzzled, and the storm stopped. Was that a permanent solution? No, there are storms to this day on the lake. But the storm was stilled for the time being. Therefore, for the time being, a person can be helped by commanding the spirit to be still. For a long-term solution, the spirit needs to be cast out of that "attacking" person.

As I speak to groups of people on this subject of deliverance, I tell them that it is important to embrace their newfound freedom and walk in the victory God has given them. He will give them that strength. One can sit under the best pastor there is, but what counts is what one does with the truths he or she hears. So it is with receiving the ministry of deliverance—it's what you do with it.

As you are journeying through this book, you may realize somewhere along the way that, in addition to strong fleshly desires that tempt all of us, there is something else troubling you deeply or even tormenting you. You may even begin to sense that it is an evil spirit. How do you get help?

Try to find someone who is being used of God in this ministry. Even if you must travel a distance to receive help, it is worth it. Some churches, even denominational churches, have a group of people who are trained in this ministry who are willing to help those in need. If you cannot find help, then I would encourage you to prepare yourself by prayer and maybe even fasting. Then, in the name of Jesus, command the spirit or spirits to leave you. Many people have been able to do this with success.

This is called self-deliverance. But I repeat, the best way is to find someone who is anointed and skilled in this ministry. If you cannot find such a person, God can meet you where you are and do mighty things!

DON'T GIVE UP!

In the world of spiritual warfare, there is a temptation for each of us to give up too easily. I remember as a third grader receiving a really nice bicycle from my parents. They were poor, and it was a sacrifice for them to purchase such a fine gift for me. I had longed for a bicycle, and now I had one! We lived on a hill, and as a beginner with little practice I mounted the bicycle and started riding down the hill. Somehow the bicycle got away from me and I crashed into an obstacle in a neighbor's yard. The bicycle was damaged, but my father was able to have it repaired. I continued to ride that bicycle for years.

I could have resolved never to ride a bicycle again. My father could have banned me from ever riding a bicycle again. But neither of those things happened. With much effort and practice I mastered riding that bike. It was not only used for pleasure because later I used it to deliver newspapers, and it was a modest source of income. As you attempt to minister to others or to yourself, you may have some "crashes." But like me, you can resolve to continue and your Father in heaven can repair the damage.

Also, in retrospect, some attempts to minister to others that first appear to be crashes really aren't crashes. Good comes out of the effort, and God is glorified. I became a better bicycle rider with the experience of the crash behind me. According to the Word of God, He causes all things to work together for good to those who love Him! (See Romans 8:28.)

QUESTIONS TO CONSIDER

1. How does Scripture define Satan?

2. What should be the primary focus of the person ministering deliverance?

3. How would you react if someone you were ministering to began to manifest in a demonic way? What should you do?

PRAYER

Almighty God, I thank You that You call us and You empower us. Teach me to come against the demonic in the authority and power of Jesus' name when I am in situations that demand it. Give me courage to confront darkness, knowing that You are with me. In Jesus' name, amen.

ENDNOTES

1. See Mark 3:11.

2. See Acts 8:7.

Chapter Five

MINISTERING DELIVERANCE TO CHILDREN

Be of sober spirit; be on the alert. Your adversary, the devil, prowls like a roaring lion, seeking someone to devour. But resist him, firm in your faith... (1 Peter 5:8-9).

...for even Satan disguises himself as an angel of light (2 Corinthians 11:14).

Our sense of fair play is offended as we begin to consider the possibility that darkness may invade youth and children. Adults? Yes. But children? It can't be! Believe me, it is very common. I would like to share some insights and suggestions I have found very helpful over the years of ministering to children.

I have found that ministering deliverance to a child is not difficult. The evil spirit has not been there for years and years as can be the case with an adult. I speak very gently explaining to the child that an old, bad spirit is trying to make him or her unhappy. I tell the child that we going to ask Jesus to make the bad spirit leave. Then, I assure the child of Jesus' love and the fact that Jesus does not want a spirit to make him or her so unhappy or troubled.

As God shows me what the spirit does to the child, I say words like, "You spirit of fear, leave my new friend." Over and over again parents will come back and testify to the real difference the ministry has made in the life of their child. Many times they want to bring a second child over for ministry. It is good to deal with these unpleasant realities while a child is young, so that a spirit is not allowed more time to gain deeper inroads into the emotions and conduct of a child. This approach is very simple, yet the results are life-changing.

Of course, there are many factors contributing to a child's development. Certainly good parenting is of prime importance. But we must be aware that darkness can be passed down through family lines. Spirits can invade a child through the sins of the parents or through some traumatic event, such as the child wandering off and being lost in the woods. In the child's panic, a spirit of fear can enter. Sadly, in our culture today, sexual abuse and bullying can also open the door to demonic attacks on our children.

Fathers and mothers whose child or children struggle greatly should learn as much as they can about the ministry of deliverance. It could be the answer to their child's misery. When I first began ministering deliverance, I did not realize that children needed this ministry. Nor did I realize fully that we have the same authority with children as we have with adults. My challenge to you, if you're a parent with a struggling child, is to pray and ask God to give you wisdom in this matter.

Be sure the youth or child is in good health. One of our children, who had a difficult early childhood, was acting out because he had serious allergies. His conduct improved as we dealt with his allergies. We live in a time of great advancements in understanding how to make the human body healthy. We should take advantage of these advancements.

Take a hard look at your parenting skills. Most parents can improve in this area. In the busy, fast-paced world we live in, sometimes we become lax in how we discipline, instruct, and interact with our children. Our number-one job as Christian parents is to raise children who love and respond to the Lord Jesus Christ. Some of us may be too lenient; others may be too hard and demanding with their children. Also, remember that each child is unique in his or her response to life, and we need the wisdom of the Lord to parent each individual child.

Shield your child as far as possible from the destructive things of life. I'm not suggesting that you be a "helicopter" parent—in the long run that does not work out so well. But I am saying that temptations in life come all too early. Children should be shielded as much as possible from these.

Most parents, both secular and Christian, attempt to shield their children from entertainment that is too intense. In bygone years, some parents were not so careful. As a four-year-old child, I was taken to see two monster movies. One was about Frankenstein and the other was about a werewolf. In retrospect, I think a spirit of fear came into me at that time. Around the age of six I saw a movie called *Bird of Paradise.* It was about a civilized man going to a Pacific island and falling in love with a young lady. In order to appease "the gods," her tribe threw her into an active volcano. It is possible that a spirit of grief came into me at that time.

It is difficult for parents to shield their children from every scary television show, video game, book, etc., but they should make every effort to do so. Even schools sometime scare young children with the celebration of Halloween, which in my opinion should not be celebrated.

With the introduction of the cell phone, Internet access, video games, etc. into our family culture, our job of protecting our children from the schemes of the devil are definitely more challenging. I strongly urge you as parents to monitor these devises carefully.

Love your children. Again and again tell the child how much you love him or her. Show by your acts of affection and care the great love you have for this gift from God. Children are slower to go looking elsewhere for love and affirmation if they receive this from their parents.

Be involved in a church that is faithful to the Lord. Also, you want the church to have good youth and children's programs. Be sure your children are involved in the programs that are available for them. Just as you take their secular education seriously, take their Christian education seriously.

While it is necessary to extend an abundance of love to children and youth, we do not make idols out of them. An idol is something that is worshiped; it is something more important than God. I have observed over the years that some parents literally make idols out of their children. The child or children run the family. Their every wish is a command to the parents. The parent lives for the child. If the parent worships the child, the child expects the worship of other people. Let me assure you, the teacher, the coach, the boss, or the future mate is not going to worship your child!

Avoid entitlement. I would go so far as to say avoid the curse of entitlement. I have seen too many young men and young women ruined by entitlement. While this is unhealthy for girls, they seem to be able to handle the parents' success better than boys. The Scripture speaks of the son who will inherit the family assets being treated as a servant. This may be too strong a demand for the twenty-first-century family, but completely spoiling a child is a recipe for heartbreak.

The pattern is clear in the business world. Oftentimes a second-generation company owner cannot give the company the success the parent had accomplished. Only a few third-generation family members manage major companies.

Barry Switzer, one of the all-time great football coaches, said the following about another favorite sport, baseball. As reported in the *Reader's Digest*, he is quoted to have said, "Some people are born on third base and go through life thinking they hit a triple." Many who are born into very successful families are tempted to believe they are entitled to all the good things that life offers. By believing this, they often become prey to the invasion of darkness into their lives because of this misconception.

What is the answer to an entitlement mindset? They should humble themselves under the mighty hand of God and seek all the help necessary to redirect their lives in God-honoring ways. Part of this help could be in the area of deliverance. Like Jesus, they should learn not to be served but to serve.

With all of this being said, how can you know if a youth or child needs deliverance? I will list a few indicators that might point to a need for deliverance:

- Driven to harm him or herself, other people, or animals

- Consumed with fear or anxiety

- Completely out of control

- Filled with hatred

- Has been sexually abused

- Sexually obsessed

- Addicted to alcohol or illegal drugs

- Obsessed with the occult

While the descriptions could go on and on, you have some understanding of what spiritual forces might be driving your child.

My parents loved each other, but they had intense verbal fights. I am sure these heated, angry battles left internal scars in my younger sister and me. I can remember blinding anger bubbling up inside of me as a teenager, which isn't good for someone trying to live a Christ-honoring life. So I adjure parents not to argue and fight in front of their children.

I think these events described were some of the happenings that opened me up for spirits to enter, which in turn caused me to need ministry as a thirty-three-year-old pastor.

I believe that the whole subject of teaching spiritual warfare and ministering deliverance are tools that no parent should be without. Two years after I began ministering in the area of deliverance, our second child was born. The focus of my ministry up to that time had been with adults. I have asked my wife to share the story of our second child:

Percy and I had just moved to our second pastorate. A few months after the move we found out we were expecting our second child. We were excited about a new baby on the way and this new place to minister. Members of our congregation began flooding my husband's office—and, at times, even our home—desiring more of the Lord in their lives. There was such hunger for God and a desire to be filled with God's Holy Spirit. Percy was not even preaching on the subject of the Holy Spirit, but the Lord continued to cause a hunger in these people. The church was growing and thriving.

After about six months of this outpouring of God's Spirit, some of the older and longtime members of the church felt very unhappy with the changes that were occurring in their church. Consequently, Percy became the object of this group's displeasure. They began a campaign to have us ousted. It was so painful for me to see my husband criticized so harshly.

I spent much time crying—being pregnant did not help with my emotions. I was very fearful at what would happen to us. It was difficult for me to see the hand of the Lord in all the turmoil swirling around us. To be quite honest, I just didn't handle the situation in a faith-filled way at all, even though there was such an outpouring of love and support from most of the church toward us. The prayer gatherings during that time were powerful and filled with the presence of the Lord. But all I could see or feel at the time was fear and rejection.

It came time for our baby to be born. The disgruntled group in the church was asking that we move out of the manse—two weeks before my due date!

The wonderful outcome is that the denomination stepped in, at the group's request, and totally reaffirmed and supported Percy as pastor. (We continued to pastor for about ten more years there.)

I had a good delivery, and our son was born perfectly healthy. But I noticed right away that when he cried, it was more of a wail—a very, loud wail. I even asked the nurse to take him back to the nursery in the hospital because of his constant, inconsolable wailing.

Even after we went home from the hospital, the wailing continued. We rarely had a good night's sleep. We tried everything, but nothing helped. I remember one particular time when I took him to our wonderful pediatrician, and told our doctor that he had to find out what was wrong with this child of ours. He assured us that our precious son was in perfect health. He said that some highly intelligent children just don't require much sleep. I quickly quipped, "Well, he's not *that* smart!"

When our son was around eighteen months old, our next-door neighbors had invited us over for lunch after church one Sunday. As we sat down to eat, our son began this loud wailing. Percy looked at me and suggested I take him home and he would eat fast and come relieve me so I could go back and eat my lunch.

As I entered our home, I suddenly was impressed that I should minister deliverance to our little one. We had been ministering deliverance now for about three years, but it had never even entered our minds that a baby might need deliverance. So I sat down in a chair and sat our child in my lap facing me. His big, blue eyes looked at me questioningly as I prayed and asked the Lord to help me. In just a normal voice, I did not want to scare him, I began to command out of him whatever I felt the Lord was putting in my mind. I commanded out spirits of rejection, fear, anger, and sadness. Our little one sat very quietly and at peace in my lap.

Soon Percy returned. As he walked in the door, I remember saying to him, "I hope you're not going to be upset with me, but I'm ministering deliverance to our son." He looked at me and replied, "That's great! You go eat, and I'll continue praying over him."

That night, for the first time in his eighteen months of life, our child slept through the night…and the next night…and the next night…. His little personality changed. He was happy and bubbly. There was no more wailing—until exactly a week later on the next Sunday. I had put him in the car seat to ride to church. As soon as I started the car, the wail began. I immediately turned to him and again in a normal, but commanding voice said to the spirit, "In Jesus' name, you cannot come back. You leave this child alone and you are never to return! Be gone!" The wailing stopped. And our child was free! Never again was he troubled by what had so tormented him for eighteen long months.

Several years later as I looked back on the whole situation, I felt like the Lord began revealing to me what had happened. In my distress and lack of trust in the Lord concerning our church situation during my pregnancy, I had inadvertently given the enemy an open door. Satan, who does not play fair, took advantage of that and attacked me by attacking my little one. I praise God for His delivering power!

Deliverance became one of many tools in our parenting toolbox with our four children. We didn't have to use it often, but when we sensed things like fear or insecurity or anger gaining a foothold in any of our children, we would pray for them in the authority that Jesus gives us as believers that they be set free. We have seen God's faithfulness over and over again!

Now let's think of how this information may apply to your children or teenagers.

Often young people become targets of dark forces. A lady in a Bible Study once asked me about an eight-year-old child whom she was trying to help. He was not raised in a cult or in a non-Christian religion. His family attended church. But often the child would repetitively declare, "I hate Jesus, I hate Jesus." If he were eighteen or twenty-eight, he may wrongly recoil at the expectations the Lord has for his life. But what eight-year-old has such a response to the Lord? Clearly, a spirit was operating within the child. The illustration I am using is extreme, I know, but it again reveals how another personality can work through a child. Can you imagine the pain those outbursts caused the parent!

Many situations are not so easily discerned as this illustration. But when children are in bondage, they need help. The family is in distress about the child; and in helping the child, the whole family is helped.

When you notice sudden, extreme changes in a child, expect a spirit. When a child is tormented, not just agitated, which is normal, or when there is unusual aggression or fear, it is very possible that there is a spirit at work. When a child, who is normal and is in good physical health, begins radically disrupting the family, it might be a spirit at work.

If you are convinced the child has spirits driving him or her, either minister to the child or find someone who can do the ministry for you.

Often what surfaces in a child also surfaces in a teenager. Many teens have added another layer of sin and destruction to their lives. These activities have opened them to other spirits in addition to what they faced as children.

They often have developed idols. Many literally worship their cell phones. It is not a tool they use—it is a tool that uses them. Other teenagers live in an alternate universe dominated by video games. Drugs and alcohol are widely used to the point that many become addicted. They will do almost anything to get their latest high.

Other teens are caught up in the sex culture. They see naked pictures of acquaintances through the use of technology. Many enter into forms of sex as early as twelve or fourteen years of age. They take crazy risks to experience momentary pleasures.

Huge pressure is put on teens to conform to group standards. If they don't conform, they are left out of the group. Or they have few or no friends. Peer pressure is extreme.

Most teenagers in past generations knew right from wrong. Many of those chose to do the wrong. But they knew it was wrong. Today, multitudes of teens have little concept about right or wrong. Consequently, many of them have opened themselves up to darkness due to their destructive activities.

A TYPICAL MINISTRY TIME WITH CHILDREN

A person in ministry and his wife brought their four young children to our home for ministry. These parents are deeply committed Christians who have been successful in their ministry. They were concerned, however, about spiritual attacks against their children, ranging in age from six to eleven. Let me share with you how I ministered to these children so you can learn how to approach the bondage in your children.

As the family entered our home, my wife and I greeted each of the children and asked them their names and ages. This is a family that, by all measurements, truly has it together. Yet, the parents sensed that some of the struggles the children were experiencing were coming from attacks of darkness. They all began by suggesting areas where darkness might be causing some of the problems. I explained in very simple terms how spirits can invade us and what might give them entrance into our lives.

Both my wife and I very calmly and gently spoke to the children. I explained to them that I was going to tell "old, bad spirits" to leave. I talked about how Jesus ministered to God's people when He was on earth and would command spirits to leave people. I reminded them of Jesus taking children in His arms to bless them. Then I prayed and broke anything of darkness passed down generationally. I asked the children in the silence of their hearts to forgive people who had wronged them and to confess their sins to the Lord Jesus.

After leading them through these preliminary steps, I then began to listen to the inner prompting of the Holy Spirit and called out spirits. My wife had several impressions from the Holy Spirit, and in agreement we also cast those spirits out. There was full affirmation and agreement from the parents to what we had sensed. I then asked the children if we had missed anything that had been troubling them. They pointed out several additional areas that were causing trouble in their lives. The parents also had several additional insights.

We prayed again, coming against the remaining several demonic holds. There was not much physical manifestation evident as we called out spirits, a few yawns and coughs perhaps. Because the spirits have not been present very long, I find ministering to children can be a relatively easy task.

The children were very willing participants and very responsive. Often, after experiences such as this, I have made new friends with children who have been brought for ministry. One might expect a negative reaction from children, but that has not been my observation.

MINISTERING SPIRITUAL WARFARE IN THE FAMILY

Parents have asked me if they should learn spiritual warfare for the sake of their families. My answer is unequivocally, "Yes." One major advantage is that by exercising your faith and your authority in Christ, you can help keep dark spiritual forces away from your family. Second, you can begin to recognize when family members or friends of your family are struggling with spiritual bondages that are hindering their relationships with others. Teaching family members about the reality of forces of darkness can help them protect themselves by their righteous conduct. It will help them be wise in what they need to avoid.

I am seeing more and more parents with young children teaching their children the reality of darkness. The children are then able to appropriate the authority of Christ and protect themselves! Parents of teenagers are bringing their teens for the ministry of deliverance. I have never heard a teenager say, "I don't believe this," or, "I don't want this ministry," or, "None of this is real." Some teens are dramatically changed for the better by the ministry of deliverance. It can free them from the destructive things that many of their peers are practicing.

I was shocked to encounter teens who had been raised in godly homes where parents had taught the dangers of the occult. Yet, these same teens or young adults had become involved in witchcraft or the occult. I wondered how this could be possible.

A parent of a girl who had been raised in a Christian home and in an excellent church had this explanation. She had observed that many times when teens go into the illegal drug scene or into the unbridled sex scene, they also encounter the occult. The occult was not what they were seeking, but they found themselves in deeper bondage than they ever thought possible. Sadly to say, while nothing is a foolproof guarantee, strong teaching in our homes can protect many family members from such destructive activities. I urge you to pray for the gift of discernment of spirits and teach spiritual warfare to your family.

CAUGHT UP IN THE OCCULT

I have ministered to several teenagers who had been caught up in the occult. I again emphasize that there seems to be a lack of awareness on the part of parents how Satan can target their children in this area. As I have previously mentioned, start from a young age teaching your children that the occult is off-limits to us who love the Lord.

I share the following story to show how two young people were swept away in deception. Admittedly, it is an extreme example, but it does show the insidious progression of evil.

A respected counseling center asked me to come alongside two of their gifted counselors to minister to a young husband and wife. Both of the counselors were experienced in the area of spiritual warfare. The three of us met together with these young adults.

They had been in serious trouble with the law. They had begun their journey as New Age participants. They soon became professionals in the New Age movement. This activity was followed with involvement in witchcraft. It is reported that they became the head of the witches of our state. This led to Satanism. At first they thought it was "cool." Next, they faced a charge of violence that produced some time in jail. After they were released from jail, they were ordered out of their community. They moved to our city and encountered a church where they were led to salvation, embracing Christ as Savior, and were baptized. A very wise pastor sent them to the counseling center, which, in turn, asked for my help.

Demons were cast out of each of the pair. We met together for three sessions. The times together were just like what happened in the New Testament. Jesus has declared that He is the same yesterday, today, and forever! The three of us witnessed the reality of this truth before our very eyes. Amazing things happened! We saw looks of torment on their faces, demonic beings stared at us from their eyes, their bodies shuddered as the demons struggled within them. But in the end, they were free! The demons left at the command of the name of Jesus!

Look ahead with me several years later. I had gathered with some of the staff and faculty to greet the new students who were entering seminary for the first time. The head of admissions approached me to say that a woman I had ministered deliverance to was one of the entering students. Wonders of wonders! It was this same young woman I had ministered to years earlier. We had a joyful reunion! She and her husband both have continued their walk of faith. He is working, and she is pursuing her master's degree with the hopes of becoming a prison chaplain.

Their story can be a powerful instrument for the Holy Spirit to use to bring many people to freedom. To go from Satanism and jail to one of the most respected seminaries in the nation is an amazing journey! It was made possible because of people who intersected their lives, believed the Scripture, and stepped out to apply the Scripture to real life. This led to freedom from a demonic stronghold, to salvation, to baptism, and now a call to ministry.

DELIVERED FROM A SPIRIT OF SEXUAL MOLESTATION

A small Youth With A Mission (YWAM) base asked me to teach on the subject of demons and how they are cast out. I asked if I could make the teaching session available to other interested people. They were agreeable with this request, so others joined us.

A businessman, whom I had not met before, came with one of his friends and sat in on the teaching and the ministry. The group was very responsive to the teaching. With their permission I closed the meeting by casting demons out of those who sought ministry to demonstrate how it is done.

Six months later I ran into this businessman at a luncheon. He told me an amazing story. He related to me that as I began to call out demons in that meeting that he thought to himself, *I don't know if I believe this or not.* As soon as he entertained that thought, God began driving something out of him. He said he felt it actually leave him.

Upon arriving at home that evening he shared this experience of deliverance with his wife. She challenged him, "If it's that good, please go pray for our daughter." Their adult daughter had been struggling greatly emotionally and mentally. Nothing in her life ever seemed to go right.

So three days later this businessman got up enough courage to pray deliverance over his daughter. She was delivered from a spirit of sexual molestation. Her life was radically changed. She was amazed at the freedom she experienced by her dad praying over her.

That incident happened over fifteen years ago; the daughter continues to do well and is free of the tormenting spirits that had plagued her for years. The businessman is now a strong proponent of this ministry of deliverance and is now ministering deliverance to others who come seeking.

Over the years I have ministered to many, many sexually abused people. In doing so, I have found that not only has great emotional damage been done, but that there is also the invasion of demonic personalities to deal with. The trauma of sex abuse allows demons to be passed from the predator to the innocent victim. Deliverance, as well as godly professional counseling, is usually needed to help the victim be freed of the great torment and wounding she or he has experienced.

A respected high school teacher came to me for ministry. This young lady had been raped by one of her students after school in her classroom. For six weeks following the horrific event she would go home and cower in her closet with a knife in her hand because of the paralyzing fear she was experiencing. Tragic as the event was psychologically, it also allowed spirits to invade her that had to be cast out. Darkness never plays fair.

I ministered deliverance, and she was set free of the tormenting spirits. She still needed professional counseling, but she was free of the spirits that had compounded her pain.

DEALING WITH A SPIRIT OF REJECTION

I once ministered deliverance to a young man whom I had only met several times. As I was preparing for the ministry time, the Lord impressed me that he struggled greatly with the feeling of not being wanted ever since childhood. After he arrived at our home, I opened in prayer and began breaking generational curses. I then began commanding out spirits that made him feel unwanted.

He looked at me incredulously and said that on the way to our home he had been thinking about how unwanted he felt all the time. He proceeded to tell me that much of the sin that had entered his life had come because of his desire to feel wanted and accepted. His father and mother had been divorced, and each had remarried. Whether real or imagined, those events left him feeling rejected and unwanted by either parent. Apparently, a cluster of spirits had invaded his life during those tragic years.

As the ministry continued, the Lord showed me that a spirit had been in his family line for generations that prohibited family members from reaching their full potential. He confirmed that this spirit was indeed at work in his own life. I broke the hold of that spirit over him and prayed that he would receive the love and forgiveness the Lord had for him. Rejection was replaced with glorious acceptance!

I have seen this spirit of rejection in children many times. Often it is present in adopted children. Other times it has gained entrance into a child because of extremely harsh words of family members, or bullying from school friends, or continual criticism leveled at the child by others. The good news is that its hold can be broken!

ADOPTED CHILDREN

Every adopted child could benefit from the ministry of deliverance. Most of these children were conceived in lust, not covenant love. The birth mother was usually filled with fear about carrying and giving birth to the child. Sometimes she was filled with anger and bitterness at the biological father who would not enter into marriage and care for her and the child.

Many times there were illegal drugs and excesses of alcohol in the life of one or both of the biological parents. In complete contrast, sometimes there were the emotions of grief and depression felt by the biological mother who had to give up the child she was carrying.

The persons ministering to an adopted child should begin by breaking generational curses, which most likely dwelt in the lives of both of the biological parents. As those ministering take the authority of Christ and break the destructive traits that have been passed down through family lines, the ministry of deliverance is now ready to happen.

INFIGHTING IN FAMILIES

Too often Christians are at war with each other. Denominations oppose other denominations. Independent congregations compete against other independent congregations. Destructive gossip is spread about fellow believers. Sometimes it is true, but it is helpful to no one. Other times the gossip is not based on truth. We see members of one group of Christians being suspicious of the successes of another group of Christians.

Even more intense than groups of Christians opposing each other is the war that occurs in many Christian families. Husbands and wives often are in real conflict. Parents and children struggle to live in the same household. Siblings who have become adults haven't spoken to each other in years. Emotional wounds from these conflicts carry on for years, if not for generations.

Is there an answer for this quarreling? I will be quick to say there are no perfect solutions for the struggles that I have just referenced. What would be a real help is for believers to recognize the source of much of this conflict is from spiritual forces of darkness. Satan has leveled these forces against believers in Christ. Based on this, if some of our energy were turned away from warfare with each other and directed against Satan's host, we would have more peace in the body of Christ. We need to know who our real enemy is and how in Christ to defeat this enemy.

A JEZEBEL SPIRIT

My wife and I once ministered to a lady who had heard us speak on the subject of spiritual warfare. Her husband is a very successful businessman; she is a stay-at-home mom with several children. Early in our conversation she related to us that witchcraft had been in her family for generations. One of her concerns was for her children. She was convinced that witchcraft had not only been passed to her by generations who went before her but also had affected several of her children. She named an occult spirit that she was convinced had invaded her. Because of this concern for herself and concern for her children she was seeking help.

I informed her that we would need three sessions together. I felt the strength of what held her would not be defeated in one session. The Lord began to give me insights into the spirits that had invaded her life. As we began focusing on the dominant spirit that she had perceived, I gave command for it to leave. I felt impressed by the Holy Spirit that this evil spirit was tauntingly saying, "You can't make me leave." We continued to command the spirit to leave. As it weakened its hold, I sensed it saying, "I will come back." By faith, I commanded it never to touch her again.

I sensed the Holy Spirit showed me that this dominant spirit had come into her life between the ages of twelve and fourteen and has been a major troubler ever since. I think her desire as a teenager to be accepted by and to control older boys was the opening the spirit needed. This particular spirit, sometimes called a Jezebel spirit, drives the person it inhabits to seduce and attempt to control people in leadership. The seduction may be sexual, or it may be emotional, or it may be economical. The person who is bound by this spirit can either be male or female, and the target may be male or female.

The name Jezebel comes from a pagan king's daughter who married Ahab, king of Israel. She clamored for her pagan god to have at least equal rights with Yahweh, the God of Israel. Part of her many acts of evil was writing letters using her husband's seal as she usurped his power. In Revelation 2:20 a woman is referenced as Jezebel. She is described as encouraging immorality and idolatry under the guise of religion.

It is sad to observe, in my opinion, that many leaders in Christianity, politics, business, and education have been brought down and their influence diminished by a person with the spirit of Jezebel. Maybe that is the reason that the Scriptures alert us not to be seduced by flattery.

Another spirit that occupies a number of people is a spirit that wants to gain power over people in leadership. The person with this driving spirit targets leaders in politics, government, business, education, and the church world. Through flattery and seduction, a person driven by this spirit tries to be a major influencer or even a controller of the person in leadership.

A MISSIONARY FAMILY RESTORED

Christmas has always been a joyful time for me! To set aside a season in the year to celebrate and remember the coming of our Lord Jesus Christ is pure joy. As a family, we have enjoyed gathering together over the years to celebrate Advent.

Another one of my enjoyments over the holidays is sending and receiving Christmas and New Year's cards. It is a pleasure to receive updates from friends and acquaintances. Of the many cards we received, a special card stood out. On the front was a picture of an accomplished family. On the back were these words, "We still treasure the memory of your kindness and the refuge of your home during our season of distress. Thank you. We find the Lord bringing us increasing opportunities to minister to others the way you did to us."

Let me give you the backstory concerning this card. A seminary professor asked me to minister to the wife of this missionary couple. The wife had a great heart for the people she was called to serve. This family had been called to minister in one of the most spiritually dark cities in the world. Without reservation, she had poured herself into their ministry to the point of collapsing. The family had to take emergency leave and return to the United States. She was admitted to Mayo Hospital, where, after an extensive battery of tests was completed, the physicians could find nothing physically wrong.

Her husband brought her and their several young children to our home. Sara Jo and I greeted them warmly as they introduced themselves to us. As the ministry began, the Holy Spirit showed me spiritual bondages in her life that I cast out. She began to manifest, showing physical signs, exactly as she had manifested in the spiritual attacks on the mission field. Both she and her husband confirmed this physical manifestation. It was a powerful and intense ministry situation. Curses over her were broken. God set her free!

You may ask what happened to them. The family is living at one of the most respected universities in the world where the husband is working on earning his PhD. She is doing very well, and, as she said in their Christmas card, they are ministering deliverance as the opportunities arise.

It is a joy to hear continued reports of freedom that people have received because of this ministry. It is a double blessing to hear that not only have they been impacted personally, but also now they are ministering to other people in the same way in which they received ministry.

SPIRITUAL HOUSECLEANING

Demons can occupy not only people, but also places. Again and again I've been called upon to minister over offices or homes that have an unexplained presence of evil in them.

Years ago I was privileged to lead a hippie couple to the Lord. The husband had been involved in a very radical college movement. Although I had invested much time in them, the young wife could never seem to get victory. I ministered deliverance to them. I counseled with them. They were faithful in church attendance. Still she did not walk in victory. She remained a very troubled woman.

With no other recourse left to me, I determined to do a "spiritual housecleaning" at their home. This was all new to me, but I thought it might be a help to the couple. They willingly invited me to their home. The couple lived in a fifty-year-old home that had belonged to her mother. I had never been in the home and knew nothing about it. As I went from room to room, the Holy Spirit began giving me a sensing and discernment of evil and dark things in the home. In the power and authority of Jesus I came against these things.

Vividly I still remember going into one particular room with the couple and experiencing a strong impression that something evil resided in a certain spot. I came against that strong spirit. When I had completed ministering and praying through the house, the wife told me in that very bedroom and in that very spot someone had committed suicide years ago. Apparently, a spirit had left the dead person but had remained in the room.

The young wife went on to be an outstanding wife, mother, and women's Bible teacher. Her husband entered Bible school. They became missionaries in Europe for six years. Then, they returned to the states where he continued to pastor in a historical denomination.

Years ago I was approached by another lady with a most unusual request. She lived in a large, lovely home with a stunning yard. From the front of the home there was a beautiful view of a stream flowing nearby. But in the backyard there was a completely barren and unsightly area.

She said that before her family had moved into the home, there had been Satan worshipers in that area where nothing would grow. She had even hired four separate arborists to do whatever was necessary to cause something to grow. They were all unsuccessful.

I asked one of the elders from our church to go with me to pray over that area. We both felt awkward, but we knew our Lord could do anything! After praying, I commanded any spirits that had attached themselves to that portion of the yard to leave.

Years later I encountered one the woman's friends who told me that the area was growing plant life wonderfully well!

The accounts could go on and on. I have been called on to pray over several companies. I would go from one workstation to the next workstation and from one office to the next office praying against any forces of darkness that may have invaded the business. We have prayed over our children's college dorm rooms; we pray over hotel rooms where we stay.

Life can be challenging enough without having a dark presence causing conflict, strife, fear, failure, etc. to harass us continually. Many times I have counseled an individual or family to take a like-minded family member or friend through the home or business and come against anything of darkness that might be causing difficulties.

QUESTIONS TO CONSIDER

1. Have you ever considered that some of the problems you face as a family could be spiritual in nature?

2. Have you had any naïve encounters with the occult of which you need to repent?

3. Have you ever considered that children could be a target of Satan? What steps could you take to help protect them from spiritual darkness?

PRAYER

Oh, Father, I cry out for my family. Show me where and how Satan has made inroads into our family structure to cause havoc. Help me to plug the gaps that have allowed him to gain entry. Teach me to minister deliverance to my children when I see that they are being harassed by the enemy. Help me to teach them how to do spiritual warfare. In Jesus' name, amen.

Chapter Six

RECOGNIZING THE POWER AND AUTHORITY OF JESUS

…The Son of God appeared for this purpose, to destroy the works of the devil (1 John 3:8).

There is one thing I would like to make clear to every reader of this book. Nothing I can do—or what other people I quote in this book can do—is possible without the accomplished work of the Lord Jesus Christ. I have sought to emphasize this truth previously, but I desire to underscore and amplify this reality still another time. While I use the name of Jesus to do this work, I hope it does not appear that I am *using* Jesus. No, rather it is Jesus who uses me! Any failures or imperfections in my ministry are my fault and my fault alone. Any successes, any accomplishments, any avenues that bring help and freedom is because, in His grace, Jesus uses me.

I have no right to use His name other than as it brings glory and honor to Him. Some readers may think of the name of Jesus as some kind of formula that helps people. I see His name as the Name above all names. I see Him as Lord of lords and King of kings. All of the names in all the earth pale in comparison to His name.

While I hope you will use that precious Name, always do so with respect for all that He has done for us. I want to do more then apply that Name to hurting people to see them helped. I want to apply the Name in such a way that Jesus receives all the glory and honor that He deserves! Therefore, I urge you to use His name in a way that people are set free but also in a way that He will receive all the glory.

Attention is given in this book to the advantages someone will discover after receiving the ministry of deliverance. He or she will find more freedom in life. This means that life will be more gratifying and more fulfilling, which is what we all desire.

Not only does the one who receives this ministry benefit from it, but the persons around the individual are benefactors also. The beings that drove the individual to be difficult are gone, and the individual is able to respond to life in a more healthy way.

But never forget that it is Jesus who made all of it possible! We contemplate the fact that the Lord left the unimaginable perfection of heaven to come to a cesspool of sin and destruction on earth—all out of obedience to the Father's will and His great love for His creation.

We are mindful of the perfect life Jesus lived. We who struggle to live a perfect day are mindful of the thirty-three and one-half years of His perfect life. Can you imagine never having an inappropriate thought, never a moment of unjustifiable anger, never a rebellious action? What a Savior we have!

We think of the rejection Jesus experienced. Many of the most powerful religious leaders of His era rejected Him. They said He was under the control of dark forces. This was said of the One who came to defeat dark forces! He endured this for our sake and for the sake of those who came before us, and should we not be the last generation, for the sake of those who come after us.

We think of Jesus' crucifixion. Most of us have never experienced the intensity of the physical pain that He endured in the crucifixion. Yet the most painful part of the crucifixion was the pain of taking on the sins of the world. None of us have any concept of that kind of suffering. He experienced all of this so that we might be a redeemed people.

Many of the hymns and praise choruses that we sing express deep thankfulness to such a Savior. Yet the greatest sacred music ever written falls far short of fully appreciating our Lord.

In Jesus' bodily resurrection from the grave, not only did He defeat death, but because of His sacrifice we who have committed ourselves to Him will also defeat death and live in heaven with Him for eternity. His glorious ascension to the right hand of His Father in heaven confirms that all He said and did was perfectly right. The ascension declared Him to be the King of kings and Lord of lords.

While the emphasis of this book is on what Jesus said and what He did, I wanted to call to our attention again the greatness of who He was and who He is today.

JESUS WARS AGAINST EVIL

There is a tendency in Christianity to pick and choose what parts of Jesus' life and ministry to embrace. This can mean that some parts of His life, ministry, and teaching are not impacting the walk of the believer. To understand fully His first-century impact, as well as His twenty-first-century impact, we need to embrace all that Scripture reveals of Him. To fail to understand and accept the deliverance part of His ministry is to fail to understand His war against evil. Some may feel that statement is unfair and unloving on His part, but He came to crush the works of Satan underfoot (see Romans 16:20). That is one of the most loving things He can do because evil causes so much pain and destruction in people's lives.

Our tendency many times is to emphasize the parts of Jesus' life that make us feel good. We can do that, but we also need to embrace all that Scripture says about our Lord. He was the Suffering Servant as revealed in both the Old and New Testaments. He laid down the glories of heaven to come to earth so that we may know God's love. He also came to break the powerful hold that Satan and his forces held over God's chosen people.

In doing so, Jesus is our perfect example. Scripture says the disciple shall be like his Teacher. Peter, James, and John were not given the option of selecting what parts of Jesus' life they would embrace. When Jesus called them to follow Him, the call was to embrace all parts of His life and ministry. When Jesus called us, His call was to accept His entire ministry as revealed in the four Gospels.

Many Christians love to focus on the baby Jesus being held by His mother Mary. His gentle and helpless nature is seen and experienced. I, too, am moved by the art that shows one of the two greatest miracles God ever performed. The Son of God is seen having taken on flesh and living among us as a helpless babe.

Another favorite scene among Christians is Jesus on the cross. As He atones for our sins, He again is seen in a helpless state. All Christendom honors His sacrifice and the awesome resurrection that followed. The resurrection was the second of the two greatest miracles that God ever performed.

Each of these two scenes, popular among artists, shows Jesus in a helpless state. Sometimes many Christians think of Jesus as being just that, helpless. He was anything but helpless for most of His thirty-three years. He spent much effort and time destroying the works of darkness with power and authority!

GOD AS WARRIOR

In Exodus 15:3 we see the following description of God: *"The Lord is a warrior...."* In the New King James Version we see, *"The Lord is a man of war...."* And Ephesians 6:12 (NKJV) tells us, *"For we do not wrestle against flesh and blood, but against principalities, against powers, against the rulers of the darkness of this age, against spiritual hosts of wickedness in heavenly places."* Derek Prince emphasized in his book *War in Heaven* that our spiritual walk is not just a defensive walk, but there is a component of offensive warfare involved. He writes, "Because our government in heaven is at war, we on earth are automatically at war, also."

As emphasized earlier, one of the great advantages in learning spiritual warfare is the advantage of being a protector to one's self and one's family and friends. In the game of football, part of the training of the athletes is to play defensively. No team ever won a football game that could not play defensive football. But the other part of the game is the offense. A team must be able to advance the ball against the opposition. If you join the team, you have committed yourself to be in opposition to the other teams that are on your schedule.

This is a somewhat imperfect picture of spiritual warfare, but it helps illustrate the point. One part of your responsibility is to protect yourself and those precious to you from attacks of dark forces. But the other part of the walk is to be on the offensive against dark forces. While we can do this in a number of important ways, this book equips you not only to play defense but to also go on the offensive against spiritual forces.

When we became part of the Lord's government, we became warriors as the Lord is described to be a warrior. Just as angelic hosts war against forces of darkness, so we are equipped to war against forces of darkness. This is part of our calling to do so.

DELIVERANCE IS A MIRACLE

I once had the opportunity to speak to a Christian university and its graduate school. The topic I chose to address was the subject of miracles. I listed six different categories of miracles found in Scripture. The sixth category I listed was that of casting out demons. This idea of categorizing the driving out of demons as a miracle was probably surprising to many of the students present. I used Mark 9:38-40 (NIV) to drive home my point. *"'Teacher,' said John, 'we saw someone driving out demons in your name and we told him to stop, because he was not one of us.' 'Do not stop him,' Jesus said. "No one who does a miracle in my name can in the next moment say anything bad about me, for whoever is not against us is for us.'"*

Four young men had accompanied my wife and me on this speaking engagement. One of the men was a successful banker, another was a physician, and two were seminary students. As I concluded my message, I gave an invitation for anyone who wanted to discuss further what I said about miracles or who desired prayer to come forward.

We were all amazed at how many of the students came forward seeking help. Each of the six of us was ministering alone because of the number of responses to the invitation. Because of my few statements about the ministry of deliverance, students came seeking prayer in the area of spiritual warfare. The Student Council that had invited us, as well as those of us who had traveled from another state to be part of this chapel service, were amazed at how God used each one of us. The few references to deliverance caused students who had great bondage in their lives to seek help. Some of them will be different people because of the ministry offered to them that morning.

TWO THRONES

The pastor of the church we attend recently preached a series of sermons entitled "Two Thrones." He drew the contrast between the Lord Jesus sitting on one of the thrones reigning as King of kings, and Satan sitting on the other throne reigning over a kingdom of darkness. He asked me to fill in for him on one of the Sundays of this series.

I spoke of Christ reigning from the throne of righteousness. Drawing from biblical information, I spoke of this kingdom being comprised of cherubim and seraphim, of angels and archangels. I referenced Michael speaking to Daniel in the Old Testament and spoke of the beautiful story of Gabriel visiting the Virgin Mary in the New Testament. I referenced ten thousand times ten thousand angelic beings existing in this kingdom.

I contrasted this kingdom of light with the kingdom of darkness. One theologian I quoted said that you cannot believe in one throne with all of its awesome beings without believing that the other kingdom exists, which is headed by Satan. In this kingdom there are fallen angels. In addition, there are authorities and powers and multitudes upon multitudes of demons. We are tempted to pretend this second set of beings have no effect on our lives. That is exactly what they want us to believe.

Our human nature is to get misty-eyed each Christmas as we again celebrate the magnificent angelic visitations to Mary and Joseph. Who can forget the multitude of angles praising God at the birth of the Christ Child in the presence of the shepherds? It is good that we are moved by these holy events. Now, that Promised One has completed His earthly mission and is seated on His much-deserved throne. He reigns now, and He will forever rule over His Kingdom.

Equally real is the kingdom where Satan sits on his throne. Equally real are the denizens that do the bidding of Satan. The purpose of these beings is to destroy the kingdom of righteousness by attacking us and entering us and causing all havoc to exist in our lives and the lives of those we love. It is the wise person who gives himself or herself fully to the kingdom of the Lord Jesus Christ. It is my hope, also, that you learn to move aggressively in the strength of the Lord against the dark spiritual forces of Satan's kingdom. It is real, but in contrast to the kingdom of Christ it will come to an end. We have the privilege of helping defeat this kingdom.

SPIRITS OF PORNOGRAPHY TACKLED

We have a large group of men from a number of churches who meet at our home one night a week. We broke our usual pattern of only men coming to the meeting by inviting several ladies to attend on one occasion. Three of these ladies are from a Christian organization that rescues children from sex slavery and women from prostitution.

I invited the ladies to speak. One of the ladies gave an eloquent presentation about girls being in bondage and the industry that held them captive. Then, speaking to the men directly, she said, "That same industry is holding some you captive." After she spoke, I invited a second lady present to pray over the men. This lady had been trafficked as a very young teenager. She escaped after six years from the clutches of this industry and gave herself to serve the Lord. As she prayed, she began to command spirits of pornography and sexual spirits to leave the men who were present. When she completed the prayer, I felt moved to continue the commands in the power and authority of Christ against demonic forces locked in any person present.

Needless to say, it was a night that will not soon be forgotten by any of us who were there. Oh, and if you are tempted to try to write this off as a group of uninformed people moved by emotions, let me tell you who was among the group: three accomplished physicians, a university professor, four bankers, a TV producer, a number of successful businessmen, etc.

PSYCHIC SCRUBBERS

In our local newspaper there was recently an article titled "Psychic Scrubbers" by Penelope Green, a writer for *The New York Times*.[1] According to the article, the "scrubber's" purpose is to fend off bad spirits. While I don't doubt for a moment that bad spirits exist, or that the people who seek these services have legitimate needs, the reality is that one source of darkness is simply being traded for another source of darkness.

While spiritual beings do exist, the psychic's attempt to drive them away is substituting one bondage with another bondage. Does that leave us helpless against forces of darkness? Absolutely not! The only legitimate force that can drive away darkness without replacing it with another type of darkness is the authority of Christ Jesus. Scripture says that He is the Light of the world (see John 8:12; 9:5). People committed to Him have the authority to command darkness to flee.

And wonders of wonders, it has to flee! Jesus, the Light, has purchased that authority by His perfect life, His sacrificial death, His glorious resurrection, and His ascension to the Father in heaven.

OCCULT AUTHORITY

A friend sent me an interesting article from *The Wall Street Journal* entitled "These Real-Life Ghostbusters Will Help Sell Your Haunted House."[2] The lengthy article speaks of people who are paid to go into houses that will not sell and drive negative forces of darkness from the homes, hoping that the houses will then sell.

One company owner paid between $500 and $750 for services for six houses that the company had listed but could not sell. Another home retailer who had twenty years of experience in flipping houses said nothing prepared her for the strange occurrences at a fixer-upper she was renovating in the Hollywood Hills neighborhood. She related, "Doors would swing open. A box of plumbing supplies moved from one corner to the other corner when we weren't looking. The floors warped for no reason. The house got broken into."

The article went on to say that a psychic medium in New Orleans who charges $200 a site visit volunteered to help an acquaintance who saw something in his house.

As you move into the area of deliverance, be equipped to give answers for situations such as these.

You may wonder what I believe about the article and some of the experiences recorded in the article. I agree with one of the people interviewed that some of the "problems" were natural and had natural answers. On the other hand, from years of experience, I also know that forces of darkness can dwell in buildings. There are different names for these spiritual entities—one is "ghost." It is my opinion that all of those beings are really demons. They just pretend to be something else.

What the "experts" are doing is using the tools of the occult to defeat the spirits hovering around a house or a building. The real answer is to apply the authority and power of the Lord Jesus Christ to the situation and in His name drive the spiritual beings away from the building where they dwell.

PINE RIDGE INDIAN RESERVATION

A sobering article was published in *The New York Times* on May 2, 2015. It was entitled, "Pine Ridge Indian Reservation Struggles with Suicides among Its Young."[3] The article reported that since that past December, a period of five months, nine people between the ages of twelve and twenty-four had committed suicide.

The article continues saying that many more youths on the reservation have tried but failed to kill themselves in the past several months: at least 103 attempts by young people ages twelve to twenty-four occurred from December to March, according to the federal Indian Health Service. Grim-faced emergency medical workers say they have been called to scenes of suicide attempts, sometimes several times a day.

The suicide attempts have come from a relatively small population. The entire reservation has a population of 16,000 to 40,000 tribal members based on varying government and tribal estimates. The reasons cited by the newspaper article for the suicide attempts are: online bullying, poverty, oppression, mental and sexual abuse, and adult alcoholism.

Another reason is also presented in the article. Several officials with knowledge of the cases said that at least one of the youths who committed suicide was influenced by "Slender Man," a tall, faceless creature who appears in storytelling websites. "They call him the 'Tall Man spirit,'" reports one of the ministers who works with youth, some of them suicidal, on the reservation. "He's appearing to these kids and telling them to kill themselves," said the minister. One of the tribal chiefs stated that many Native Americans believe in a suicide spirit similar to the Slender Man.

Ten men from our community recently went on a mission's trip to Pine Ridge. Four of the young men who made the trip have attended meetings in our home. They affirmed the accuracy of the article. There is a serious spiritual condition in play here, as well as a socio-economic situation. Could Native American youth be seeing something? I cannot say, but what I can say is that Satan and his hosts are behind this destruction of human life.

But there is power and authority in the name of Jesus to break this hold and deception perpetrated by Satan himself. From what we understand, many Christians are reaching out to the Pine Ridge Indian Reservation.

WE HAVE BEEN GIVEN AUTHORITY

James Scott writes in a history of World War II about the amazing rescue of 707 prisoners of war held by the Japanese.[4] These prisoners had been terribly treated: starved and severely beaten. When Japan surrendered to the Allies, the U.S. Navy realized they had to rescue those desperate prisoners as soon as possible. Commodore Roger Simpson was commander of the rescue operation. His chief-of-staff was Commander Harrell Stassen.

When the party arrived at the prison camp, the Japanese guards were armed with fixed bayonets. Simpson, Stassen and some of the American officials were taken to the Japanese colonel who ruled the prison camp. When told to release the prisoners of war, the colonel said he did not have orders from his war department to release them. Simpson countered that Admiral Halsey had ordered the immediate liberation of the prisoners.

"I have no authority to release them," the Japanese colonel stammered. "You have no authority, period!" Stassen fired back. The allies, led by the U.S., had won the war. The commander knew he was on the winning side. Because he was on the winning side, he had the authority to free the captives!

This powerfully illustrates our situation today. Because of Christ's victory we are on the side that has the authority to command the release of the captives!

JESUS TODAY

I again emphasize the important truth that Jesus' primary ministries were to preach the kingdom of heaven, cast out demons, and to heal the sick. To that end, I quote a scholar, R. T. France, in his commentary on Matthew: "His [Jesus'] ministry will begin in the context of a call to repentance from sin (Matthew 3;2,6;4:17), and while the focus of that ministry will be on teaching, healing, and exorcism, He will also assert His authority on earth to forgive sins."[5]

That brings us to a current-day question. If Jesus had delayed and waited nearly two millennia to come to earth, what would His primary ministries be? I believe His ministry would be much like His first-century ministry. Since the modern world has many hospitals and medical professionals, Jesus may have left some of that ministry to them. But I believe that He still would have emphasized His preaching and teaching ministry and His deliverance ministry. I base that, in part, on the Scripture that declares, *"Jesus Christ is the same yesterday, today, and forever"* (Hebrews 13:8).

QUESTIONS TO CONSIDER

1. Do you feel you are becoming better equipped to move aggressively in the strength of the Lord against the dark spiritual forces of Satan's kingdom?

2. Had you ever considered that Scripture indicates that deliverance is a miracle?

3. What examples could you give that demonstrate that our society today needs the ministry of deliverance just as much as the church of the first century?

PRAYER

Father, there are so many desperate, hurting people around us. In the natural we can see what is happening, but give us spiritual eyes to see the war raging around us. Help us know when to war spiritually. Thank You that You really are the Warrior. Thank You for all that Jesus did on the cross that we might be victorious in this spiritual battle. And thank You that You are the same yesterday, today, and forever. In Jesus' precious name, amen.

ENDNOTES

1. Penelope Green, "Cleaning More Than Cobwebs," June 5, 2013, *The New York Times;* https://www.nytimes.com/2013/06/06/garden/scrubbing-the-house-right-down-to-the-vibes.html; accessed August 21, 2019.

2. Katy McLaughlin, "These Real-Life Ghostbusters Will Help Sell Your Haunted House," October 27, 2016, *The Wall Street Journal;* https://www.wsj.com/articles/these-real-life-ghostbusters-will-help-sell-your-haunted-house-1477578503; accessed August 22, 2019.

3. Julie Bosman, "Pine Ridge Indian Reservation Struggles With Suicides Among Its Young," May 2, 2015, *The New York Times;* https://www.nytimes.com/2015/05/02/us/pine-ridge-indian-reservation-struggles-with-suicides-among-young-people.html; accessed August 22, 2019.

4. James Scott, *The War Below* (New York: Simon & Schuster, 2014), 306–307.

5. R.T. French, *Matthew: An Introduction and Commentary* (Downers Grove, IL: IVP Academic, 2008), 54.

Chapter Seven

PERSONAL TESTIMONIES OF FREEDOM

...Now have come the salvation and the power and the kingdom of our God, and the authority of his Messiah. For the accuser of our brothers and sisters, who accuses them before our God day and night, has been hurled down. They triumphed over him by the blood of the Lamb and by the word of their testimony... (Revelation 12:10-11 NIV).

The following are a group of stories about the ministry of deliverance in the lives of people we know and trust. They serve in places of leadership in our communities and in our churches. They come from a wide variety of church backgrounds. These stories are written in their own words. They have enriched this book by their courageous accounts of God at work in their lives.

Those who have written their accounts were offered the opportunity to remain anonymous. We have honored those requests of anonymity. Many, many more could have written of their encounters with the ministry of deliverance with excellence. Maybe those are for a future book.

These freedom accounts are important because they can be faith-builders for you, our dear reader. In the fight against the powers of darkness, testimonies hold an important and powerful place. The Scripture quoted at the beginning of this chapter says, *"They triumphed over him* [the devil] *by the blood of the Lamb and by the word of their testimony."*

It is hard to deny the reality of this ministry when one reads the stories from these capable people. It is surprising that, upon being asked to write their stories, not a one of them refused.

While I or both my wife and I were involved in each of these ministry situations with one exception, we do not want to take the credit for ourselves. The real truth is that Christ deserves all the thanksgiving and all the praise for what He has done in each of these lives. It was His love, expressed through His authority, which impacted and changed these precious lives. I am sure that each of these storytellers would also be quick to give Him their deep gratitude.

Let faith arise!

A MOTHER OF FOUR

"Percy and his wife, Sara Jo, are gifts to the body of Christ. I have seen God use their ministry and teaching as a resource to all denominations, people of all occupations, families of all sizes, and followers of Christ in all seasons.

"Although I had heard much about their deliverance ministry before I met them, I first met Percy and Sara Jo because they were chaplains of a long-standing leadership training in our city. I was matched with Sara Jo in the mentoring program; and through this program, I was first welcomed into their home. There I was given one of my first books about spiritual warfare. Percy and Sara Jo helped me grow in my understanding of what the Bible teaches about the invisible war and how to rebuke the enemy and his tactics for myself and my family. They prayed over me and ministered to me in these first sessions together, modeling the ministry of Jesus. They listened and loved every time I entered their home.

"That was just the beginning. I have been welcomed into their peaceful home over and over again throughout the years for discipleship, prayer, deliverance ministry, and Bible study. In any major transition in life, my husband and I have sought their wisdom and ministry. They have embraced my family during hard times and led us to God's grace, the power in forgiveness and the ministry of the Holy Spirit. They have taught us how to recognize the strongholds of the enemy and how to be set free, emphasizing that God always has the last word. They have encouraged my husband and me in our own ministry and have given us the tools to walk out Jesus' ministry of healing and deliverance with others.

"As a mother of four, it has been a joy to see my children appreciate Percy and Sara Jo's loving approach and teaching as well. They have hosted our entire family for both a meal and ministry time. Percy and Sara Jo have also come to our house for a time of prayer over our children and home. Percy has shared some powerful words of knowledge about each one of my children and parenting insight during these ministry times. He has gently and calmly walked through deliverance ministry with my children.

"Additionally, Sara Jo has always been there, adding her wisdom and writing notes in order for reflection afterward. We have gone back to those words (both positive and negative) multiple times as we seek to raise up world changers who follow Jesus all the days of their lives. We have also implemented this ministry in our home, teaching our children what Percy and Sara Jo have modeled for us. My husband and I also have the benefit of seeing the fruit of their home; Percy and Sara Jo have amazing children and grandchildren. Love abounds in their home.

"Beyond personal ministry times, they also lead group studies or prayer times. Recently, I was able to sit under Percy's teaching in a Bible study. Of course, we were welcomed into their home, and we opened God's Word together. We went verse by verse through the Gospel of Luke and other parts of Scripture. Percy opened up a time for Q&A during every meeting to get into some real-life examples and practical, how-to teaching. The women in this study were built up and encouraged. It was a profound time of equipping the female side of the body of Christ.

"All in all, my life has been changed. I have seen power in Percy and Sara Jo's ministry because they operate out of the overflow of God's peace, the abundance of the Father's love, the discernment of the Holy Spirit, and the solid teaching of God's Word. May they continue to be used to teach and model the ministry of our Lord and Savior Jesus Christ."

A FORMER TV EXECUTIVE PRODUCER SEEKS HELP

"The stress of running those shows and handling the underwriting produced a constant battle for me. One day I told Carole, my assistant, how miserable I was. Carole said, 'I have a suggestion for you. Maybe your struggles are spiritual in nature. Maybe you need to have a total cleansing of any demons or curses that may have attached themselves to you. I know a pastor here in town who can cast out demons and break curses.'

"I immediately had visions of Linda Blair in the movie *The Exorcist*, and the thought that I might be possessed with demons scared me to death. But I was so miserable that I told Carol I would go. She set up the appointment. I immediately called my sister to go with me, because I was afraid to go alone, but I was determined to go if it meant that I could solve my problems once and for all—even if it involved having Satan's little henchman driven away.

"My sister and I met on Monday morning at the church. As we entered the pastor's office, the receptionist instructed us to have a seat, and said the pastor would be with us shortly. Reverend Percy Burns was in his office with a young man who was in training to do the same type of deliverance ministry that Reverend Burns was called to do. They were in there praying. My heart raced as we waited. I thanked my sister for sitting in on the session.

"It was time, and we were called into his office. Percy sat there, relaxed, with the young man who was in training. He then began by explaining what the casting out of demons was, and how often Jesus had done it in the Bible. He said he would be going through my life, from childhood to the present, with the Holy Spirit's help to find any ways that I had been exposed to demonic forces. The gentleman assisting him would be both praying for us during this time and recording whatever was discovered through what the Spirit told them.

"Percy would then, with the Holy Spirit's help, remove any demonic influences or curses resulting from various things, including innocent games we may have played as a child, things like the use of a Ouija board, holding séances, consulting horoscopes and psychics, etc.

"My sister and I were stunned. We had done a number of those things as children. We had thought it was just play not knowing that it was a serious offense to God. We hadn't realized that we had been attempting to do something that only God could and should do as He alone knows the future. At that time, we did not have Bible knowledge to know that we were committing a sin. To be honest, I had forgotten that we had even participated in such things until he asked us if we had ever played with any of them. We always thought it was harmless play. Satan used it against us. He often uses ignorance to get us to open the door for him.

"Percy said that different people respond in different ways when a demon is cast out or a curse is removed. Some people just open their mouths and yawn. A few may scream, and some may even throw up. I looked at my sister; and she looked at me. I wanted to run out of the room. This was pretty serious stuff we were about to do. I became a little frightened. I did not want to throw up in someone's office. Percy then asked my sister if she wanted to be cleansed as well. My sister's reply, 'I want to do anything that will bring me closer to God.' So there we were. There was no backing out now.

"Percy began by praying. I immediately noticed the change occur in his face. He closed his eyes while communing with the Holy Spirit. He was allowing the Holy Spirit to give him information he might need to know about our lives and family history, and what, if any, demons or curses needed to be dismissed. He began telling me about things that had happened my childhood. I looked at my sister and thought, *How does he know all this?* Every time he was right on the money.

"He began dismissing demons and calling them by name. The ones that seem to be a problem for me produced a yawn in me. Thank goodness, we were not screaming or throwing up on the floor. He prayed for the forgiveness of our sins and asked God that we be cleansed and released from generational curses in the name of Jesus. My sister later told me that she kept blowing out and yawning because she didn't want any demonic forces in her life.

"Later, my sister explained to me that Christians who have the Holy Spirit living in them couldn't be possessed by demons, only harassed by them. And even then, we can command them to flee in Jesus' name. But many Christians struggle with even believing that demonic forces can be responsible for things in their lives, or that they can harass the people because of choices they have made. Satan made sure that movies and stories distort the truth and desensitize us. We don't study the Bible enough, and churches often don't teach about the dangers around us. We can look around the world today and see evil at work. It's funny how we don't often see the evil that may be within us."

A CHRISTIAN COUNSELOR EXPERIENCES FREEDOM

"Early on in my journey of healing from a painful childhood, God impressed on me Jesus' words in John 8:32 (NIV), *'Then you will know the truth, and the truth will set you free.'* I never could have known how far-reaching that verse would become in my life!

"I had the privilege of meeting with a Christian counselor under whose guidance I healed from my troubled past. Through that process I learned about counseling and felt God leading me to become a counselor. I wanted to see others set free as I had been. Again God's Word spoke to me. In Luke 4:18 (NIV), Jesus explained, *'The Spirit of the Lord is on me, because he has anointed me to proclaim good news to the poor. He has sent me to proclaim freedom for the prisoners and recovery of sight for the blind, to set the oppressed free.'* And once again, I had no idea of the depth of meaning those verses held for my life.

"So I changed careers and became a licensed mental health counselor. I was enjoying my new profession and saw God at work in the lives of clients, but God still had much to teach me.

"A close friend told me of a prayer ministry at her church by a pastor with a spiritual gift of word of knowledge and deliverance. As she explained this to me, I was fascinated. Coming from a background of believing the impossibility of a Christian having a demon, I wondered why deliverance would be necessary. In my limited exposure to deliverance, I thought of such words as *exorcism* and the movie *The Exorcist*, even though I had not seen that movie.

"However, hearing my friend's testimony of this type of ministry in her life resulted in the desire that this gentleman pray for me. Still, at the same time, I was frightened as to what God might show him about me and what would happen in the deliverance part. Nevertheless, I arranged for a prayer time with this pastor, Percy Burns.

"The results were amazing. God obviously revealed to Pastor Burns things in my life he could not possibly have known. Then, as he commanded out demons, a deeper level of healing occurred. The spirits of darkness were replaced with the fruits of God's Holy Spirit. I was filled with peace, joy, and so much more energy.

"A few weeks later I asked one of my colleagues if she had noticed any difference in me and she said, 'You are not always saying how tired you are.' Another colleague said she had noticed 'more enthusiasm in my work.' The demonic influence had siphoned off my joy and a lot of my energy and definitely the abundant life that Jesus promises in John 10:10 (KJV).

"As I began to realize the new depth of healing I had experienced, I immediately thought of my counseling clients and wanted them to experience this aspect of healing. There was a spiritual aspect of healing of which I was previously unaware, and I wanted to know more.

"I began to read and study and learned that the King James words 'demon possessed' are better translated as 'demonized,' i.e., having a demon. Demonic spirits can gain a foothold of influence in a Christian's life, but Jesus gave His disciples *'authority to drive out impure* [evil] *spirits and to heal every disease and sickness'* (Matthew 10:1 NIV). That same authority is available to us today through the power of the blood of Jesus; and at the name of Jesus, the demons are commanded to leave!

"I continued to work with my counseling clients in traditional ways but also began to recommend that clients address the subject of spiritual warfare in such areas as forgiveness, ancestral sins, spirits of fear, rejection, anger, and so many more.

"I have had the privilege of directing and accompanying clients to persons who minister deliverance to Christians. It is always amazing to me to watch God working in lives of clients at a deeper level of healing than can be accomplished through counseling. Miracles that can only be attributed to God happen through the ministry of deliverance.

"As Dr. W. Appleby writes, 'God has provided deliverance for His people so they can be set free—released from demonically driven thoughts, behaviors, and emotions. God wants His people to be free from such things so that they can serve Him more perfectly.'[1]

"I remembered the passage in Luke 4:18-19 (NIV) that God had impressed upon me when I became a counselor. I wanted those who were oppressed and prisoners of their circumstances to be set free, but I had no idea of the spiritual warfare, i.e., deliverance, involved in that process. Thanks be to God that He guided me further into the deeper meaning of this verse.

"I think back to John 8:32 (NIV), *'Then you will know the truth, and the truth will set you free.'* I confronted the truth in my own life through counseling and gained a huge level of freedom, but it was the truth about deliverance from demonic influence that *fully* set this captive free, as well as so many others with whom I have had the privilege of coming alongside."

—A Christian counselor

MY PACT WITH THE DEVIL MADE NULL AND VOID

"I was raised in a committed Christian family who regularly attended church, but I began to stray from my faith during my junior year of high school. When I entered college, I joined a fraternity and started partying hard-core. Six to seven nights a week we would get black-out drunk and smoke marijuana. It was in one of those blackout states that voices started entering my mind. They would speak horrible things to me and put grotesque images into my brain.

"With my religious upbringing, I knew that Satan existed, but I had no clue that I was opening myself up to his antics. Nor did I comprehend that there was such a thing as spiritual warfare. So I stayed in denial that the voices might be demons and blamed it on the alcohol and drugs I was using. But deep inside of me I knew that I could not write all of this off to hallucinations. Something else was warring inside of me.

"During my junior year of college one of the voices began asking me about this girl I really liked. She had never really paid much attention to me, but I had the biggest crush on her. The voice said, 'If you serve me, I'll give her to you.' So in my altered state of consciousness, I agreed. I believed that God had turned me over to Satan anyway, so I might as well go down that path.

"About a year later this girl moved several doors down from our house with her friends. One thing led to another, and over the course of events we ended up sleeping together. After that night, in fact the very next morning, the girl dumped me completely and never wanted anything to do with me again. The realization hit me like a ton of bricks. I remembered the agreement I had made with darkness a year before—I had made a pact with the devil and had lost!

"I graduated from college and, through a series of God-ordained encounters, God began to pull me miraculously from Satan's grip. I began crossing paths with men of great faith who began teaching me the power of the blood of Jesus. I learned that I had entered into a contract with Satan and that it had to be broken by my confession of sin to the Lord and asking the Lord Jesus for mercy and forgiveness. I proclaimed my salvation in Christ, pleading the blood of Jesus over me, and informed Satan that our contract was severed in the powerful name of Jesus.

"In my journey back to the Lord, the Lord began delivering me from the demons that had so plagued me. One night as I lay on my bedroom floor, I actually felt some of them leave as I cried out to God. Other spirits had to be cast out by people who had a strong ministry in deliverance. Still others came out as I walked through forgiveness of others and confession of sins that lay buried deep within me.

"If you are reading this and have ever entertained or been comforted by strange voices in your mind, or if you have ever made a mental or verbal agreement with Satan, I plead with you to fall at the feet of Jesus immediately and cry out for His forgiveness and mercy immediately.

"I have learned much about perseverance these last several years—persevering in prayer, persevering in taking every thought captive, persevering in walking in His joy, persevering in spending time in His Word and in His presence. Thanks be to Jesus that every day when I worship and pray and spend time in His Word, I experience even greater freedom. The Lord has given me a beautiful wife, and together we look forward to bringing glory and honor to Him. I *know* that the good work He started in me *will* be completed!"

—A successful young businessman

FROM SHAME TO FREEDOM TO MINISTRY LEADER

"In the late 1970s, during renewal services at our Presbyterian church, I was exposed for the first time to the ministry of deliverance. However, it was not until I met Percy Burns that I was able to begin to learn and understand this ministry both for myself and for others.

"Percy's ministry had and continues to have a tremendous impact not only for me but for others. His heart to teach and mentor others is a powerful gift to the body of Christ. His teaching on deliverance was the key the Lord used in the journey of bringing inner-healing and freedom into my life.

"During a mid-week church service years ago, Percy stated, 'Anyone who has had a lot of trauma in life is a candidate for deliverance.' Having grown up in a family of alcoholism with all its effects of deep fear, anger, confusion, insecurity, legalism, performance, etc., I thought, *Well, I certainly fit that category.* But, like so many others, I was afraid and ashamed to admit that I needed deliverance. However, it soon became very evident to me that I was desperately in need of this ministry.

"From Scripture I learned the reality and importance of this ministry. I saw that Jesus spent so much of His time ministering deliverance, and I learned how the enemy uses situations and sins in our life to gain demonic strongholds.

"When I did make the call to set up my session, Percy's way of ministering with such gentleness, yet powerful authority was very comforting to me. He broke generational sins over my life, as well as word curses and lies the enemy had planted in me. I asked the Lord to search my heart for any unconfessed sin and for any unforgiveness I might harbor. I was blown away as this pastor told me about things that had happened in my life that he had no way of knowing and how they had become open doors for the enemy to gain strongholds. I knew the Holy Spirit was at work.

"After several sessions of deliverance, I was experiencing deeper and deeper freedom. I was delivered from a spirit of shame that had so overwhelmed me. At some point Percy encouraged me to do self-deliverance when I felt the onslaught of the enemy. I began to do just that. Through the powerful name and authority of Jesus, I began to cast out spirits. I called him later to report, 'Hey Percy, it worked!' He let out his 'whoop' that is so familiar to us all. What a wonderful memory; I was being gently pushed out of the nest so I could begin to move into this powerful ministry.

"Because of the ministry of deliverance, I am now living a life of freedom that I never thought I would or could experience. The pain, the legalism, the insecurity and fear, the self-condemnation—the list could go on and on—that so plagued my life has been dealt with. I learned how to keep my deliverance, because the enemy does not want us to stay free. I needed to be prepared to take authority over any spirits that tried to come back and to stay close to the Lord.

"Then late one afternoon the enemy played his hand. The Lord let me spiritually see three dark figures walking toward me. I immediately discerned what spirits they were. Rather than panicking, I just said, 'No, you cannot come back—in Jesus' name, be gone.' They left! It was a powerful lesson and one I have shared numerous times.

"I have been blessed to be mentored by Percy over the years and value the opportunities to sit in ministry sessions with him. Several years ago, the Lord led several of us to begin Aletheia Ministries, which is an inner-healing and deliverance ministry of our Presbyterian Church. Percy serves on the board of this ministry.

"Percy's faithfulness to the Lord's calling on his life and his leadership and influence through the power and authority of Jesus Christ just keeps on impacting lives. Lives are turned around and set free. He continues to mentor and raise up others in this ministry of deliverance, that is so needed today."

—A businesswoman and ministry leader

DELIVERANCE FROM DRUG ADDICTION

"Eleven years ago I was battling a very intense drug addiction and was hearing voices. I enrolled in three different rehabilitation centers, visited secular counselors, Christian counselors, psychiatrists, medical doctors, and was hospitalized a few times. NONE OF THESE PEOPLE COULD TELL ME WHAT THE VOICES WERE! I was angry! I wanted to punch someone in the face! I was struggling with something that was real, and I wanted to know how to get some relief!

"I would inform these professionals that I was hearing voices. The only answer I got was that it was called 'psychosis' defined by the American Medical Association (AMA) as 'not real, a form of hallucination, disconnected from reality.' However, I knew that what I was dealing with was real! Furthermore, when I was honest with people and told them the truth of what I was dealing with, they would recommend that I be moved to a psychiatric treatment center or mental health hospital and treated with heavy doses of sedative drugs. I knew without a doubt that this was not the answer for me.

"Finally, after years of struggling and searching for answers, I ran into Pastor Percy Burns and simply asked him if he would pray for me. He did, but then a few weeks later he invited me to come visit him for a time of praying for spiritual warfare, something having to do with curses and demons and such. I said, 'I don't believe in all that nonsense, but I've tried everything else and nothing has worked, so I'll give it a try.' However, there was part of me that had considered the fact that I really could be dealing with something supernatural.

"During the visit, the pastor and others members of his church graciously prayed for me and led me through a series of steps including:

1. Personally confirming my salvation

2. Humbling myself and repenting and confessing known sin

3. Forgiving others

4. Breaking generational curses and any involvement with the occult

5. Breaking spoken curses over my life by me and others

6. Breaking personal, unwise vows

7. Casting out demons

"I did not have an immediate reaction during the three hours of intense prayer, but later after I returned to my hotel room, I was tired and felt like I had just run a marathon. When I lay down on my bed to rest, the instant that I began to doze off, my body began trembling. I was awakened to feel myself cough several times. Except it was not a cough, not even a sneeze—it was something else. I could physically feel pieces of breath expel from my throat and mouth.

"This happened over and over again every time that I would begin to fall asleep. After about forty-five minutes of having these pieces of breath leave me, something like the turning on of a light bulb in my mind happened. I had clarity in my head that I had never experienced before. I felt a cool, clear breeze run from one ear to the other inside my head as if my brain were being wiped clean of viruses, similar to a computer's hard drive.

"I opened a book that Percy had given me titled *They Shall Expel Demons.* As I read it, I looked up every reference to Scripture in the book. I realized that Jesus and all the followers of Jesus, including the disciples and apostles and many others Jesus sent out to do His work, were commanded to cast out demons. At this point I realized that what I had been struggling with for years were evil spirits. The Bible says in John 8:32 that '...*the truth will set you free.*' Praise the Lord, I indeed had just found the truth. It was right in front of me the whole time in the Bible.

"From that point forward I have been free from hearing voices, free of addictions and self-destruction. Although over the next few years I had a few 'falls,' each time I knew how to deal with the recovery process and was able to get freedom again.

"Now, as I look back eleven years later, God has done an amazing work in my life. I have been to Israel eight times, volunteering with ministries such as the International Christian Embassy in Jerusalem (ICEJ). I have spent extended seasons at the International House of Prayer in Kansas City (IHOPKC). I serve as a leader on the intercessory prayer team at Passion Conferences with sixty thousand college students in attendance. I have worked for some great ministries like Derek Prince Ministries. I am heavily involved in my church and have served as a deacon. Currently, I am enrolled in seminary and plan to be a pastor soon. Praise God! The truth has set me free and I plan to serve *Him* as long as I have breath in this body!

"Jesus and His Word, the Bible, are the only answer to our problems. I respect the professionals in the medical world, especially when I need antibiotics or surgery. But there are some things that can only be addressed with the spiritual weapon of deliverance. God has given me a vision for future ministry, and I now minister to those who hear voices and who are oppressed with demonic forces. God is using me regularly to cast out evil spirits from people who are struggling with oppression. God is so good! I know now that He has been preparing me for the greatest struggles that this world has ever faced as we approach the end of time. I see that spiritual warfare is essential to live the Christian life, especially in the days ahead!"

—A seminary student

A WONDERFULLY CHANGED YOUNG MAN

"June 27, 2014, is a day that will live in the recesses of my mind forever. This day was a game changer when it came to how I viewed myself, others, and practices—and most importantly, God Himself. It was a day that set off a surge of hope and clarity that wouldn't have happened if I had balked at the Holy Spirit's leading.

"To give you a brief background of why this date is so important to me, I must rewind to mid-February of that year. During this time, I experienced spiritual, mental, and relational trauma. Within a matter of days, two guys from my church turned their backs on me; I received a traffic ticket, which resulted in a hair-trigger meltdown on Facebook; and I ran into issues with one of my anti-anxiety medications. Needless to say, I was left feeling stressed, exhausted, sad, and even a bit paranoid. I felt like nobody understood me anymore. I literally felt like I was headed for a mental breakdown at any moment.

"Over the next several months, all of these pains started to attack me during the most vulnerable time for any human being, my sleep. I have struggled with getting quality sleep for most of my adult life; and my sleep went into a deep decline. I began to have very vivid, exotic dreams of being involved in various sexual encounters with men. This vicious cycle repeated itself at least three or more nights a week. At first, these dreams felt really good. It didn't take long for these dreams to dissolve into more violent sexual episodes.

"The dreams eventually stopped attacking me while I was asleep; however, they started to attack me as I was going to bed. No matter how many sleeping pills and anxiety pills I took, those same-sex sexual dreams found a way to rev up in my mind as I was trying to rest. It got to the place where I stayed up for up to ninety minutes to make those dreams and voices stop before I could go to sleep. I even contemplated having an actual sexual encounter with another man, hoping that it would cease the nightmares. It was only by God's immeasurable grace that this never happened.

"By now, I was depleted. While I knew deep down that Satan was viciously attacking me, I just had no more energy to combat him. I thought that God had totally abandoned me. I came to the conclusion that I just better learn to live with this oppressive albatross for the rest of my life.

"Now back to the morning of June 27: a dear friend and I met at the home of Percy Burns. I walked into Pastor Burns' home feeling a hybrid mix of anxiety, hope, fear, anguish, and curiosity. A quick note: Percy Burns has been blessed with a supernatural, indescribable gift of inner healing and deliverance.

"Over the course of the next one and a half hours, the way that the Holy Spirit ministered to me was so transforming and indescribable that it just gives me chills and tears thinking about it. Anyway, word curses, generational curses, and spirits surrounding my same-sex sexual dreams, worry, anxiety, fear, depression, etc. were exposed. Each were renounced and broken in the name of Jesus. Words of life, hope, joy, and peace were spoken over me to replace the destructiveness that had permeated most of my life.

"As my friend and I left the Burns' home, I knew that something had shifted, but I couldn't figure out what it was. I felt as though a trillion pounds of oppressive weight had been lifted off my shoulders. I felt like God finally had paid attention to the many nights of tears, anguish, and torment that I had endured the last several months. And most importantly, I found I could be vulnerable and transparent without fear.

"Ever since that day, the way I view myself, others, and God has dramatically changed in several ways:

1. Since that day at Percy Burns' home, those same-sex sexual dreams (and the fear of having them) disappeared that very same night and haven't been back to visit me as of this writing!

2. I've been able to put my sexuality in a better and healthier perspective. As the Lord told me recently, "You may have same-sex (sexual) desires, but they no longer have you!" These desires no longer have the ability to dictate my life. I can confidently say, 'I'm not gay,' with full sincerity.

3. I know that the touch of a man that I was craving wasn't going to be in the bedroom, but in the form of brotherhood where I can be loved, encouraged, and corrected—a place where I know that I'm one of the guys.

4. More importantly, I've felt more intimate with and closer to God than ever before. My sleep is now a peaceful place where I can experience God's voice of affirmation and love. I am beginning to learn what it means to exercise the authority that Jesus died to give me.

5. I realize that I am fearfully and wonderfully made. I am His and He is mine. I am made in His own image and His own likeness. I am His!"

MY DELIVERANCE FROM A SPIRIT OF FEAR

"I was raised in a family of ten children who went to church every Sunday. Sadly, the emphasis in our denomination was a salvation by works and not a personal relationship with God. As a teen, I became hungry for more and began searching for the truth. I even traveled to California, hitchhiking and sleeping in parks and beaches, in my quest. No cult or religion was off-limits in my search for freedom and truth, and yet I became more and more in bondage.

"Fear and panic attacks began happening frequently. My life was soon spinning out of control, and no amount of meditation would help. Eventually, I decided to end my life. With gun in hand, I remembered the words of a street preacher I had met in my wanderings. He had told me, 'When you come to the end of yourself, call on God.' I noted that he said 'when,' not 'if.' I put the gun down, got on my knees, and asked God to help me like the street preacher had said.

"Several weeks later, someone invited me to a prayer meeting to which I declined. However, this young man asked me every week for several weeks until I finally gave in. As we entered this prayer meeting, there was praise and worship, and I could feel something I could not explain. At the end we all joined hands in prayer. A great conviction came upon me of the terrible sinner I was. I feared greatly that I would die in this state. I cried out, 'Jesus, save me!' I felt an incredible peace fill me and knew that my life had changed.

"As time went on, the Lord was faithful to lead me to a wonderful church where I could grow in the Lord. He surrounded me with Christian brothers and sisters. Life was good. However, the panic attacks did not go away. They were not as frequent, but they would still happen. Fear would grip me, especially in crowds. In childlike faith I asked God to help me, and in His faithfulness He did.

"A Christian brother gave me a popular Christian book on demons and deliverance, and I read it cover to cover. I realized my fear attacks must be demonic in origin. But not knowing anyone who did 'deliverance ministry,' I could only ask God if He would provide me a way to be set free. Several weeks later He did.

"Late one evening while sleeping, I woke to find myself suffocating. It felt like someone had placed a wet mattress on top of me and was pressing down. In my panic I cried out to Jesus to help me. At that moment, His presence came into the room. I could make out His outline, and He was surrounded by light, although I could not describe in detail His appearance. He spoke to me clearly, 'Behold I have given you authority over all the power of the enemy.' I began to rebuke this thing that was suffocating me. I would find temporary relief, but then it resumed. It went back and forth like this several times. I cried out, 'Lord, why can't I get it to go?' He said, 'How can two walk together lest they be agreed?' Instantly I was convicted that somehow over time I had begun to accept the fear and even enjoyed the adrenalin rushes it provided. Immediately I repented and shouted, 'I break the agreement!'

"The demon left, and at that instant I saw two bloodshot animal-like eyes look into mine and then flee. I asked the Lord how that thing had entered me, and He gave me a vision of me sitting and meditating to a guru several years back. I saw a smoke-like wisp enter me as I sat with my eyes closed. This is a lesson to the dangers of dabbling in false religions.

"Over the next several weeks, I had an episode when my heart began to race, and I feared that it was coming back. A wise Christian brother told me it was normal for the demon to try to return after being cast out. He advised me to begin praising God whenever I sensed that happening. I did just that, and it would leave. After a few more attempts that resulted in a praise session, the demon never came back. I have been free from fear ever since.

"After my deliverance, God gave me boldness to share my faith. Many of my family members received Christ after seeing the dramatic change in my life. My mother even received a miraculous healing after suffering several back surgeries that had left her in constant pain and almost bedridden. The doctors could not explain it.

"About fifteen years after I had received deliverance, I sensed the Holy Spirit speaking to me that one of my sons had the same spirit of fear that I had had. He had always been an extremely shy child, especially around people he didn't know well. As he grew into a teenager, he did not outgrow this shyness. It actually became worse to the point that he was a very fearful young man.

"When he was around fourteen or fifteen years of age, the Lord prompted me to cast out a spirit of fear from him. Regrettably, I had never taught any of my children about spiritual warfare, but I went to him and asked him if he wanted not to be shy anymore. With him in agreement with me, I prayed for him and cast out a spirit of fear in the authority of Christ.

"There was no visible manifestation; everything was calm and peaceful. But my son changed overnight! He was a different person. He joined the debate team soon after this event. During his college years he participated in an internship out of the country. He now has a great job. That spirit of fear and shyness that plagued him for so long is gone!

"Over the past forty years, God has been faithful to do many wonderful things in my life. My experience has been that the Christian life is not without trials and suffering, and most are not demonic in origin. However, when they are, we can praise God that *He has given us authority over all the power of the enemy* (see Luke 10:19)."

—A successful businessman and church elder

A YOUNG PASTOR'S TESTIMONY

"First of all, I want to say that Percy Burns has been and continues to be a tremendous blessing in my life. If you were baptized in the Holy Spirit after a time when you previously thought your Christian walk without this baptism was well and good, you will know that it's like the difference between hearing about the glory of a World Series championship as a child and then growing up and playing for the winning team! This is what Percy gave to me in the Lord, to experientially walk in God's victory.

"I got to know Percy shortly after beginning seminary while participating in a prayer meeting. During the meeting, Percy paused and said something to the effect of, 'I hear the Lord saying He has a unique calling on your life. You have been living in the world long enough, and it is time to take Him and His way seriously. Today He is blessing you with a new awareness of His presence.' At that moment, I felt this heavy weight come upon me gently, yet thoroughly, that led me to get to my knees. I did not know what the glory of the Lord was at that time, but I was experiencing a manifestation of a facet of that glory. I also did not know that God still spoke, and I was in a state of amazement! And then I was filled with joy and a sense of rightness that has not left.

"Soon after, I knew that God had more for me. I called Percy, and he was gracious in making time to meet with me for one-on-one prayer. This time he began to minister deliverance to me. He called out many aspects of my life that I had struggled with, but from which I did not know I could be free. One of these was second-guessing myself. 'I discern a spirit of second-guessing that has been oppressing you. I command this spirit to leave and I drive you out in the name of Jesus.' It was a calm and simple prayer, without drama, and led to a subsequent experience of a gentle peace and quiet resting both in my mind and within my emotions.

"In the days that followed and ever since, my decisions have been definitively more decisive. I have had almost no anxiety and little regret concerning decisions I have made, compared with years past.

"Percy continued, 'I call out a spirit that intimidates you around strong-willed women. I discern this has been passed down from your father's side. In the name of Jesus I come against you and command you away. I drive you out. I break the curse of intimidation of women in the name of Jesus and bless you with confidence in Him as a male.' Again, calm, confident, and simple.

"What Percy did not know at the time was that my father and mother's relationship was one characterized by her aggressive will and his passivity. I believe it is preferable for women to be strong of character rather than weak, so this is no commentary on that quality, but rather one of observing a non-supportive quality in my dad. I, too, had inherited that quality, and if you were to ask my wife, she would say that since that time I have grown much in my leadership within our relationship and am able to better support her own strength instead of incorrectly feeling intimidated by it.

"I could give you many more examples of this as Percy has helpfully and healthily delivered me from dozens of demonic spirits in the name of Jesus. He most often will have a Scripture verse to support the renewed mind that is necessary to build upon the deliverance. With deliverance he builds a foundation for discipleship.

"For me, the true test of the fruit of Percy's ministry is that I am now helping set others free and watching them grow and walk in freedom. I have witnessed many, many others do the same over the years that I have known Percy. As has been said before, this city is blessed to have Percy Burns as a pastor."

FREEDOM FROM A TURBULENT PAST

"Having been raised in a non-Christian home in Colorado, I would say that I was fully immersed in a lifestyle where I had become a product of worldly living. My parents had an unhealthy marriage that was volatile in nature and provided an unstable home environment. My father had an unhealthy dependence on alcohol through my middle-school years. My mother experienced severe depression and was suicidal from my middle-school years through college when my parents ultimately divorced. My relationship with my only sibling, my older sister, was distant and strained due to competition and the fact that she felt I was favored by my parents.

"My father was in the military so my home environment was extremely rule- and performance-based. I became a superstar at achieving love through performance. I was a straight-A student and had worked my way onto a three-time national champion soccer team that led me to a prestigious academic institution on a soccer scholarship. I was a survivor of a school shooting incident that killed many classmates and left our community in the wake of destruction. To say the least, I was thoroughly looking forward to getting away from the weight of my youth in Colorado and finding new experiences and successes in college!

"From an outsider's viewpoint, I was 'on the right track'; but in reality, I was a wreck. Emotionally, I was standing on an ever-shifting and unstable foundation of achievement and approval-gaining. Two events eventually forced me to consider whether or not I could really 'control' everything in my life: my parents' divorce became final and a severe injury in soccer sidelined me from playing. I now praise God for the women He divinely placed on my collegiate soccer team who welcomed me to church and made concerted efforts to speak to me about Jesus. I accepted Christ at the age of twenty and I started to learn about grace.

"Concurrently, I pursued years of counseling to sort through the emotional collateral that was the result of my upbringing and found it supremely challenging to 'overcome' many behaviors that were developed out of my circumstances through the years. Despite heavy investments in counseling, I was still unable to free myself of the challenges experienced in my upbringing and the emotional bondage that encaged me in various ways.

"Though the facts of my childhood and youth may sound harsh, I want to confirm that in no way do I blame any resulting output of my upbringing on my parents. They did the very best that they could right where they were, and I very much honor their guidance, love, and support throughout my developmental years and on into my adult years. My faith, combined with the counseling I received, provided a solid platform for restoration of relationships, as well as forgiveness.

"I moved to a new city to pursue a master's level program at a seminary. This is where I first met Percy Burns who was serving as chaplain of the seminary at the time of my matriculation. He and his wife, Sara Jo, had also ministered to my childhood best friend from Colorado and her husband, who coincidentally now lived in this city, and she had been telling me about the phenomenal impact of their ministry for years. She encouraged me to seek them out for freedom from the bondage I very obviously couldn't resolve myself. At that point, life had thoroughly worn me down; I was in desperate need of some hope, and I finally chose to pursue ministry from Percy and Sara Jo. I picked up the phone, dialed the number that my best friend had given me, and scheduled a visit to meet Percy at his home.

"From the second that the front door swung open, I felt an overwhelming sense of peace sweep through me. Percy and Sara Jo's home seemed to be filled with light, tranquility, and solitude. These things were notably evident to me just walking into their foyer, and it served as confirmation that their home was where I should be. My best friend had accompanied me to Percy's home, and as we sat to speak, he shared his background of how he had stepped into the deliverance ministry. He then asked me if I had any questions. I had already exhausted my best friend with questions prior to the meeting, so he stated that he would lead in prayer. He explained that as he recognized any spirit, he would name it, bind it, and cast it out in Jesus' name. My best friend joined him by taking notes and agreeing with him in prayer.

"Admittedly, I was shocked at how many spirits Percy cast out of me that evening. However, as our time of prayer rounded down, I felt true transformation when Percy led me into the baptism of the Holy Spirit. Looking back, that would prove to be a pivotal moment where the trajectory of my life was altered.

"Others began to note specific changes in me who had absolutely *no* clue about my time with Percy. Someone who had known me for years told me that they noticed I was much freer in social settings, as if I had come into my own. Ironically, Percy had cast out a spirit of the 'little girl' accompanied with anxiety that came from my mother's side. My mother has always struggled with social anxiety, and I had taken on this as well. I also noted that the first time I went to the library to read for seminary, that I was devouring the Old Testament. Previously, I had to backtrack and reread as I struggled to retain the content of the Bible and was always distracted by random noise or whispering in the library. In reflecting on this, I recalled that a spirit of distraction in reading and learning had been cast out.

"I had always been able to read people extremely well. Not just slightly or that I had a good sense about someone, I could usually pin them down—and quickly. That night Percy cast out a spirit of the occult and stated that I had the ability to read someone in a supernatural way. He stated that it was not of Christ. I was petrified! I took great pride in being able to understand people well; almost immediately I could get a feel for their intentions and know their stance even when it wasn't communicated in words. Percy was telling me this trait was not of Christ and that it was a spirit of the occult. I don't think I could have been more shocked.

"Over the course of three additional visits, Percy cast out many other spirits; all of which were spot on and directly aligned with things I knew to be true about myself. Noticeable changes were occurring in many areas of my life. There was absolutely no way he would be able to know these things about me or even from which side of my familial line they originated in the flesh.

"I continue to be astounded at the Lord's work. Percy's gift of discernment to identify and recognize the spirits that captivated me in bondage is miraculous. I have been able to move beyond many of the challenges that once held me enslaved emotionally. Behaviors that I simply could not rectify myself and overcome have been broken off and sown into my past. I have experienced a freedom that could not have been imagined in advance, because I had come to see this bondage as 'normal' and just something that I would have to deal with the rest of my life. I will be forever grateful for the ministry of deliverance in my life."

—A young businesswoman

A LAWYER'S PERSPECTIVE

"My family has experienced firsthand the miraculous gift of deliverance. With a host of known generational behaviors, the travails of divorce, and untold supernatural attacks, my sons were exhibiting the effects of oppression from evil spiritual forces. So we scheduled a time where the whole family could meet with Percy and Sara Jo.

"Perhaps the greatest tribute to the Burns' family is the very presence of God that is experienced as soon as the threshold of their home is crossed. Not only is their home welcoming and cozy, but it is a sanctuary filled with the Holy Spirit. So after some small talk and visiting, we got to work praying for each one of the children. Much like my first experience with deliverance, the Holy Spirit shone a spotlight on the issues and challenges that had plagued and were plaguing them. Just like every member of a family has a unique personality and spiritual giftings that fit into the larger theme of the family, so it goes with respect to spiritual attack and generational curses. There may be common threads associated with the experience of the family as a whole, in our case a hurtful divorce, but each individual was also dealing with their own unique spiritual assaults that seemed to line up with their personalities.

"I wish I could say that after one night of intense prayer that our family was freed and never wrestled with any of those challenges again. But in our true-to-life experience, the results were only somewhat apparent, and it would take a significant ongoing investment of prayer and positive choices to head our family in the right direction. But as we mounted up on that narrow path, we walked with the benefit of an established course and bearing that had been set that evening in the Burns' home—a path of godliness and good choices that would see our family through.

"Since that night, we have had challenges innumerable, and they have been intense. We have dealt with the enemy's expert infiltration and the inherent challenges of raising teenage boys in a digital world. My oldest son has dealt with the challenges of dyslexia, ADHD, and professionals who placed him on the autism spectrum. He has also been the most adversely affected by the divorce. These challenges were exacerbated with the onset of puberty, and notwithstanding our best efforts to the contrary, we watched him become increasingly sullen as he wrestled with all the feelings inside him. He frequently drew dark pictures and seemed like he was depressed or angry almost all of the time.

"When he turned twelve, I asked him if he would like to attend with me the men's Fire Group which meets weekly at Percy's home. I thought it would be a good way to expose him to godly men and show him what that looks like firsthand. My real hope was that he would experience the deliverance and infilling of the Spirit that overflows in abundance on Monday nights. The first night he was there, after I gently redirected him past the distraction of the hot tea machine and the book about WWII, he settled on the couch close to the music.

"After a couple of songs in, he started to harmonize in the Spirit, bringing the angelic voice with which he has been blessed as a welcome accouterment to the worship leader's guitar and the other deep voices of the guys. As he sang, I started to silently weep inside with gratitude for what the Lord had done and how far He had brought my son and my entire family.

"Later that night my son told me about the visions he was having of a butterfly, and that he felt like the Lord was showing him the butterfly as a special message to him to appreciate life. The transformation was nothing short of miraculous. It was like a switch had been thrown!

"Over the next few months, we regularly attended the Fire Group, which meets at Pastor Burns' home. Sometimes my son would sing and sometimes he got distracted, but the effect on him was nothing short of amazing. During that time, I also kept hearing from people about how much his singing had blessed them. The child I had been most concerned about was inspiring others in their worship! He has also started writing kind letters to his brothers, telling them that he cares for them and that he wants to get to know them better—this from the same kid who used to stomp them if they crossed him!

"He continues to be challenged by the stuff that all teenagers face, but instead of days of sulking about something, with a little redirection he returns quickly to a young man who understands the grace he has been given by Christ. Through my son I have seen the power of deliverance and the infilling of the Holy Spirit firsthand, and my family has experienced the miraculous effects that it has had on both him and me. For this, words do not exist to express the extent of my gratitude."

AN ATTACK OF DARKNESS OVERCOME

"Our four-year-old son was sleeping in a big-boy bed and was just starting to get up in the morning on his own and start playing without us. If a parent, you may remember those young childhood years. You know what a blessing those times can be on a Saturday morning. We could finally lie in bed just a few extra minutes and listen to him playing happily without us. We also had a two-year-old daughter. She was content to wake up and entertain herself in her crib for a short while before calling us to come get her.

"It was a Saturday morning scene much like I just described. We lay there awake in bed listening to our children play, when our son walks into our room, toy in hand. In a totally calm, completely matter-of-fact voice, he said, 'I just wanted you to know that the gray man is here. He's watching me play, but I didn't look at him or talk to him. I just wanted you to know.' And then he turned and casually walked out to go back to playing.

"What?! Gray man?! In our family room watching our son play? What?!

"I jumped up to investigate, but I was the only one rattled. I found our son happily playing as if nothing was unusual at all. After a few more questions, it was clear to me that he could see someone and something that I could *not*. This was not his imagination. He was not pretending, nor was he shaken.

"That was the beginning of a whole new kind of 'activity.' The 'gray man' encounter was nothing compared to the other things that he would see. He started calling me during the night, telling me, in vivid detail who and what he could see and the things they were saying to him.

"Our children attended a Christian preschool and were well versed in Bible stories and who Jesus was and is. They knew what it meant to accept Jesus as Savior, and could speak of Him in detail. These nighttime visitors our son had would tell him things about Jesus too—things like *Jesus isn't real.'* Or, *'If Jesus is real, why isn't He helping you now?'* Or they would just taunt him incessantly with chanting or playing eerie music—making him cry and beg for them to stop.

"I couldn't hear them, but I believed my son. His descriptions were too vivid and too full of details that he would have had no frame of reference from which to fabricate them. He would tell me exactly what they were saying, like a translator. We would pray. They would stop, and he'd finally be able to go back to sleep.

"These occurrences got more and more frequent. These weren't nightmares. He wasn't asleep. He wasn't dreaming. These things were waking him up and then tormenting him. During the next year, we moved. I had high hopes that whatever was causing all of this was related to that house, and that we'd be leaving it behind.

"But shortly after moving into our new home, the incidents began happening again. The new home wasn't really *our* home. We were renting it while we found a place to build our new home. The room our son was in had a large window in the middle of the wall that was the 'bed wall' so to speak. It was two windows wide and each went nearly to the floor and nearly to the ceiling. His bed was a bunk bed. Though it wasn't the best spot, it was the only wall large enough for his bed, so we placed it across in front of the windows. We locked the windows, and put shades that stayed down over them so it didn't seem quite as 'open' to the outside.

"As was fairly common, my son called me during the night because *they* had arrived. Only this time it was much more serious than any other time before. Since the move, our son had been sleeping on the top bunk. When I walked in, he was sitting on the edge of the bunk on his knees, facing the window, rocking back and forth, telling me he didn't want to jump. He was crying, not hysterically, but crying. He asked me if I would jump with him. I didn't know what he was talking about. He said, 'They're telling me to jump. I don't want to jump. Jump with me, Mommy.' Of course, I grabbed him and held him tight. We came down from the top bunk and I told him he didn't have to jump. We prayed. They left.

"As I tucked my son back into bed, I felt the need to check the window, so I raised the shade. Much to my surprise, the window was open! These were double-hung windows—which means they were the kind that slide up and down to open and have a lock in the middle where they meet. When unlocked, you can either slide the top section down or the bottom section up. The top section of the window was unlocked *and* open. It was only covered by a thin pleated fabric shade. That top open section was nearly even with the edge of that upper bunk where my son had been rocking on the edge when he called me.

"This room was on the second floor of the house. I know my son would not have known how to open that window. It would have been difficult for him to get to it. He would have had to raise the shade, unlock the window, then figure out how to slide the top window down, and then go back down and lower the shade again to cover it. Why? Why would he do that, since he 'didn't want to jump'? These visitors were trying to coax my now five-year-old son to leap from a second-story window to his certain death.

"I'm sure you can surmise that we had now quickly moved into that state of pure desperation to help our child. The episodes were increasing in frequency as well as severity. Nearly every visit was yet a new way of trying to convince him to harm himself. One night, he was at the top of the stairs and talking about jumping over the balcony rail. Another time he was standing at the top of the staircase as if waiting to be pushed down the stairs, which were a long set of wooden curved stairs that would have definitely caused serious injury if not death. These things were out to get my son! I couldn't figure out who they were, nor why they were there.

"But God.

"In a series of divine appointments, I found myself sitting with my son, meeting with Reverend Percy Burns. Percy is a soft spoken, retired Presbyterian pastor, and one of the most calm, mild-mannered, unassuming men I have ever met. It didn't take long for both of us to understand what had been going on in our house as Percy gave my son and me the biblical foundation and scriptural evidence for demonic activity. We knew, and Percy knew, that we had surely been dealing with demons. But what we learned next in that meeting changed everything!

"We learned that we had authority over them in Jesus' name; that at the name of Jesus, they had to flee! This was new. They had been leaving when I prayed, so I already understood the concept on some level. But I hadn't been commanding them to leave. I'd simply been praying for comfort or peace or the presence of the Lord. So, yes, it caused them to leave temporarily, but they always returned. I hadn't been telling them they had no rights to be there. I hadn't understood the authority we have as believers. I hadn't prayed with belief, only out of desperation. But now Percy had given me solid truth that the same power that rose Jesus from the grave was at our disposal if we believed in Him as Savior (see Romans 8:11, Ephesians 1:19-20 and Ephesians 3:20).

"My son seemed to understand as well. He knew how real his experiences had been, and so did I. We needed no convincing of that. But there was still a puzzle piece missing—the why? Why were they bothering my son? Our family?

"As Percy prayed for us, the Lord gave him wisdom that only He could have given—things about my family ancestry that were linked to the demonic activity we had been experiencing. They were things I knew to be true, but I had no idea that they could have any effect on my family or me or bring demonic activity into our family. There were curses and family strongholds. The Holy Spirit revealed specifics to Percy that I had not told him or anyone. I began to realize that these demons were on assignment to kill my son.

"Within a few days, Percy and his wife, Sara Jo, came to the house we were renting to do a spiritual housecleaning. In hopes of identifying more specifically why these demons had chosen our son and seemed so relentless in their pursuit of him, we spent a great deal of time in my son's room.

"Percy asked me if something had happened to my son when he was born. Had he been sick or almost died or anything? I hadn't told Percy a thing about his traumatic birth. But the Holy Spirit began revealing to Percy that somehow through the events at his birth there had been an open door to the demonic. So, as it turned out, our experiences had been a spiritual attack from darkness itself. And that is why the doctors could not trace the lack of breathing to any medical cause or condition.

"Percy was impressed that the demons most likely would try to come back to harass our son. But the thought of them returning wasn't scary or unknown anymore. We knew what we were dealing with, and we knew that we had full authority over them through the power of Jesus.

"The demons did try to come back, but our disposition and our state of mind had changed dramatically. I commanded them to leave in Jesus' name. I spoke with confidence against them, even though I could not see or hear them. I told them that my son belonged to the one true and Holy God of Abraham, Isaac, and Jacob. I would tell my son to proclaim the name of Jesus as well. I would have him tell them to leave in Jesus' name. In the beginning, he would always want me to do it with him or do it first. He would tell me that they didn't listen to him. I explained to him that he must speak it *and* believe it because he has authority as a child of God.

"By the time he was in the third grade, he was much more confident in believing that he was fighting from an unshakable position of victory. All that we had experienced as a family allowed for a very open dialogue about what was going on and how we handled it. Our daughter doesn't remember a time that we didn't talk about the power given to us in Jesus' name.

"I recall a conversation on the way home from school one day when my daughter was seven or eight years old. She was talking about a fear or a bad dream she had had the previous night. Before I could respond, my son spoke up and explained to her to just say the name of Jesus out loud when she was afraid. He told her to cast down anything that was causing fear in Jesus' name. He went on to tell her that he used to feel uncomfortable doing it himself, but that he wasn't now, and that she could do it too. That's a priceless blessing!

"His depth of belief continued to grow. He learned about Martin Luther in school. They had to memorize the speech that Martin Luther gave at the Diet of Worms that launched the Protestant Reformation. He walked around reciting the speech constantly. But there was a particular legend of Martin Luther's life that really resonated with him. It is said that Martin Luther received frequent visits from demons and Satan, particularly while he was working on his Bible translations and during his stay at the Wartburg Castle in Germany. He would get all worked up praying, singing, and shouting at the evil spirits to leave him alone.

"As the story goes, these dark visits continued until one night Martin Luther was awakened by them, but he had become so confident in the power of God being stronger than the demons, that he simply lifted his head from his pillow, saw them at the foot of the bed and said, 'Oh, it's you again,' and laid back down and went to sleep. That's Christ confidence at its best!

"If there is anything for us to learn from my testimony and my family's life experience, it's that we should not guard our children from the full counsel of Scripture and we should trust them with God's truth—the complete gospel, the full power of Jesus and the Holy Spirit from day one. It is a normal part of what the disciples did, and, I believe, it should be just as normal in our households. Trust me, your children are likely to receive it and grab hold of it without thinking a thing of it. May the word of my testimony strengthen and encourage you as you prepare your children for their service in the kingdom."

—A stay-at-home mother of two turned servant of the Lord,
prayer warrior, and women's Bible teacher

AN ENGINEER'S JOURNEY

"For me, getting involved in the ministry of deliverance was more of a process that revealed itself as I went along rather than a deliberate path that I chose. God prepared me, shaped me, and then empowered me to minister to those facing spiritual oppression and the influence of demons in their lives. Throughout the preparation stage, I became more and more aware of the spiritual battles that take place all around us and of the reality that there are specific forces of evil. During this shaping process, God brought people into my life who had faithfully served in the ministry of deliverance.

"One of those people was the Reverend Percy Burns. The Lord used him to teach me and help shape me into a leader in the ministry of deliverance. First, Reverend Burns taught me the biblical basis for deliverance ministry, and then he ministered to me in the area of deliverance. Through the process of receiving deliverance, I was also blessed to receive an infilling of the Holy Spirit like nothing I had ever experienced before. This was all part of the process of preparing, shaping, and empowering me to serve in the wonderful area of ministry.

"I like to say that if I can be a leader in ministering deliverance, then so can anyone else God chooses to call into this ministry—regardless of their background, their denomination, etc. It is God who handles the preparation, shaping, and empowerment—we must only trust in and depend on the Lord to provide all that we need. It is with this trust and dependence that I slowly stepped onto the path that brought me to opportunities for ministering deliverance. To better appreciate the emphasis that God uses all types of people in ministry, but especially in the area of deliverance, it is helpful to understand my background.

"I grew up in a loving family, but I left the church at a very early age and began to wander aimlessly as I sought a multitude of things this world has to offer. As I began to seek a deeper meaning and purpose for my life, I turned to military service. I spent several years being conditioned to respect discipline and to find fulfillment in serving others, not for my benefit but the greater good. My horizon was expanded as I learned about the world beyond my rural upbringing. Throughout this process, God led me to seek higher education. I completed my military service and began my college studies. I was able to finish my undergraduate and master's degrees in engineering. This, in turn, opened a door for a career in engineering.

"I will fast-forward a few years with a few highlights. When our first child was born, we nearly lost him. I cried out before God to have mercy on my son, and in that process God was more real to me than ever before. It was, in its essence, my conversion experience. Years later I found myself living in a new town and wrestling with a call to ministry. I did not know where it was going to take me, but I found myself speaking to God as I drove down the freeway, releasing my will and seeking His as I committed to enter seminary.

"As I began my seminary training, I began to realize just how much I did not know and how little I truly understood about the spiritual warfare that we all face every day. I was blessed to be enrolled in a non-denominational seminary that enabled me to interact with and become great friends with people from many different backgrounds. Some were very similar to my own, and some were quite charismatic in their worship styles.

"It was a beautiful time of my life, and I was blessed beyond anything I ever deserved. It was also a busy time of life as I continued to work as an engineer with more than fifteen years' experience, plus take seminary courses. There was not much free time, but every class was enlightening; there were many times when I felt that I had just completed a full day of worship rather than a full day of class time!

"As I began to grow deeper in my relationship with the Lord, I began to experience things outside of the classroom that I could not explain with the traditional theology of most mainline churches. I recognized we are called to trust and obey rather than understand and control, but there were times when I did not know what to do with information that I received in ministry settings.

"In one particular situation, what I was hearing from the individual was not stemming from a natural problem, but rather a supernatural one and I did not know how to minister to this person. Prayer and Scripture reading helped, as did the good counseling techniques of effective listening. But there was something more that needed to be done. There was something very lacking in my approach to ministering to this person. I needed to get help, and it was with this in mind that I sought the help of one of my great friends.

"My friend listened to me and showed no signs of shock or surprise. How could this be? All of this was quite new to me, and it was quite clear that the ministry opportunity that I had been presented with involved the embodiment of evil—an evil being. This was way beyond what I had ever experienced, but my friend seemed hardly phased by it. He listened patiently, asked me a few questions, and concluded that the scenario was legitimate, and that I should seek guidance—which is what I thought I had done in coming to him! In love and understanding, he directed me to meet with Reverend Percy Burns. This is how one of the greatest times of spiritual growth began in my life!

"Percy sat with me and patiently listened to all I had to say, jotting a few notes and listening both to me and the Lord as I talked about all that I had experienced leading up to that meeting. Then he began teaching me about demons and their torment in the lives of people. He was leading me through the Scriptures, and it was on the truth of Scripture that he taught me, blessing me as he did so. Then he began to minster to me as the Lord led him, and he began to take authority of evil spirits that were active in my life. He identified things by name that he had no way of knowing other than by divine revelation.

"It was amazing, enlightening, freeing, wonderful, draining, and even troublesome at times because I thought that I had overcome some of the things that he was calling out. Thankfully, Percy was very gentle throughout the process. It was obvious that the power of the Lord was revealing these things to him. It was also obvious that the power of the Lord was driving them out of me as Percy spoke in a calm voice and trusted the Holy Spirit to do the work.

"We had several sessions like that, and each time Percy would give me a list of things to pray over. Also each time, he would pray over me to bring in a fresh filling of the Holy Spirit. Each time I would go away with a warming of my heart that I could not explain. On our last of such sessions, we prayed together for me to receive the baptism of the Holy Spirit. I also received the gift of discernment that God uses to reveal demonic activity to me.

"Over the ensuing years, I have led several deliverance ministry activities helping to identify the evil spirits that are active in people's lives, calling on the name of Jesus and the blood of the cross to take authority over the spirits and drive them out of the people to whom I was ministering. This is such an important area of ministry, and I thank God for the opportunities that He has presented to me. The church needs this ministry today as much or even more than it did in the past. Our culture is overrun with sin, and there are so many gateways to spiritual darkness that we all too often open without having any idea of the evil that lies at the roots.

"It was with this in mind that I responded to the Lord's prompting to write a small guidebook that prepares people to recognize the need for the ministry of deliverance and the importance of keeping this ministry firmly grounded in the truth of God's holy Word. I owe a tremendous debt to Percy for his patient and wonderful guidance through the truth of God's Word as it relates to the importance of deliverance. I have used this guidebook to teach a couple of classes to people who may have never thought about the need for this ministry, and I pray that they have all benefited from the study of God's Word as we explored the topics together.

"For all who are reading this and may have been inspired to step out in faith and respond to God's calling on your life in the area of deliverance ministry, I encourage you to follow your calling in determined obedience, always depending on the Lord, always trusting in Him and not your understanding. He will bless you beyond anything you could ever imagine and, more importantly, He will bless others through you and your obedience to respond to His calling on your life."

QUESTIONS TO CONSIDER

1. The Scripture passage in Revelation 12:10 states they *"triumphed over Satan by the blood of the Lamb and by the word of their testimony."* In what way(s) can our testimony cause us to be triumphant over Satan?

2. Did any of the testimonies help build your faith? Which ones?

3. Are you more encouraged to believe that Jesus, indeed, came to set the captives free?

PRAYER

Oh, Father, You are indeed almighty God! With You, nothing is impossible. Thank You that You came to set the captives free, that You are the same today, yesterday, and forever! Thank You for the changed lives and families these testimonies represent. I look to You to move in my life and in the lives of my loved ones. In the powerful name of our Deliverer, amen.

ENDNOTE

1. David W. Appleby, "Deliverance as Part of the Therapeutic Process," an address to the American Association of Christian Counselors, September 15, 2007.

Chapter Eight

QUESTIONS YOU MAY HAVE

And when He had come into the house, His disciples asked Him privately, "Why could we not cast it out?" So He said to them, "This kind can come out by nothing but prayer and fasting" (Mark 9:28-29 NKJV).

As you begin to integrate the ministry of deliverance into the fabric of your Christian walk, you may find that questions arise that cause you to ponder. Hopefully, I can address some of these questions in this chapter.

WHY ARE MORE PEOPLE SEEKING HELP?

Why are more and more people seeking the ministry of deliverance? I believe there are several reasons for this. First of all, people are really hurting. I do not have to tell you of the overwhelming number of people inside and outside our churches who need help. I do not have to belabor this point because we all know it is true.

It also has become apparent to us that more people are having dreadful experiences in the night, which cannot be written off to bad dreams or vivid imaginations. After someone has seen a scary figure appearing during the nighttime hours, the person is often ready to seek help. While some of these phenomena have existed for many years, it seems to me that these kinds of unholy encounters are happening more often.

Parents are increasingly seeking ministry for their children. Children are encountering more darkness in our schools, colleges, and universities. In addition to this darkness, consider all that they are encountering through the Internet. Godly parents are trying every way possible to find help for their precious children.

There is also increasing distrust and conflict inside of marriages. Many couples, because of vows they have taken before the Lord or for the sake of their children, are trying desperately to remain together in a productive way as husband and wife. After having tried everything known to them, they are now seeking the Lord's help through the ministry of deliverance.

Other people simply know that they are not living out the life described for them in Scripture. They are trying very hard to be set free from the overbearing weights of life in order that they can be what God has called them to be. It is very difficult to live the kind of life pictured in Scripture if there are spirits lodged in them misdirecting their walk.

IS DELIVERANCE BECOMING MORE ACCEPTED?

I believe the modern believer in Christ is more open to the reality of spiritual warfare than were believers in the last century. There are several reasons for that trend. First, they have not been as misguided as were many believers several generations ago. The prevailing mindset then was that the concept of spiritual warfare was superstitious or illogical. Others taught the reality of the demonic in first-century Christianity but felt it had little meaning for their generation. Science was paramount. The prevailing opinion was that science would solve most of people's problems given enough time and resources.

Today, with the collapse of so much in our society that we once held sacred, people are awakening to the reality of dark forces destroying individuals, families, and even churches. There is a heart cry for God's help. People are humbling themselves and recognizing that destructive forces have worked against them and even sometimes through them. The pride that once drove so many people is now being abandoned because of their own personal needs.

God can move in these situations that I am describing, and God is moving in the hearts of the humble. We can't afford to let intellectual snobbery keep us from the blessings of the Lord. Trying to impress others with our so-called intellect and worldly wisdom can rob us of the freedom that God has for us.

A GREATER NEED FOR DELIVERANCE NOW?

While I believe that every generation since the New Testament times has needed the ministry of deliverance, I do believe that those of us living in the Western world have an increasing need for this ministry.

As I have said more than once in this book, there are many theologians of different persuasions who believe that at the end of the age there will be a great outpouring of demonic forces. An unholy release will take place throughout the earth. God's creation, especially those created in His image, will be the target of this outpouring of evil.

In the face of what many understand Scripture to say about end times, the church has at least three options. While this end-time prophecy might take place in a decade, or a century, or a millennium from now, how the church responds to the present darkness may be an indicator of how the church will respond in the future to more intense darkness.

The church could choose to live in denial. It could pretend that nothing of darkness is happening. In contrast to what our news media is telling us each day, there are some in our churches who will not acknowledge the reality of what is occurring in our culture.

On the other hand, the church could just simply "wring its hands" in despair. In the face of the great sins of humankind and the work of dark forces, portions of the church live in hopelessness. "Since we can't do much about it, we will just survive" is their mindset.

The third option the church has is to respond courageously; moving in the authority merited by our Lord Jesus Christ and testified to by the Word, the church could make a real difference! That surely had to be the philosophy of the New Testament church. With God's help, we won't live in denial and pretend everything is all right. We won't wring our hands and feel like we are hopeless. Instead, we will move forward in courage, with faith-filled expectation of victory over darkness!

Those of us who live in the Western part of the world have certainly had our share of spiritual darkness. But in recent years we are seeing an increase of that darkness as people from some of the most spiritually dark places in the world are coming into our countries, even into our communities. Along with some of these people come dark spiritual forces. This statement is in no way a position on the issue of immigration. It is simply an attempt to wake us up to the spiritual realities our communities continue to face. These facts offer both opportunity and challenge.

If many theologians are correct in their thinking that there is to be a great outpouring of darkness at the end of the age, will the church be ready for such an outpouring? Will we, and those who come after us, be prepared for spiritual warfare? We can only answer that question for ourselves and for our families.

WHY DO DEMONS FRIGHTEN US?

Most expressions of the Christian faith believe in the existence of Satan. He is introduced to us in the early chapters of Genesis as we have seen. There are glimpses of him in the Old Testament. We have a more vivid understanding of him as we read of him resisting the work of the Lord Jesus in the Gospels. Information continues to come to us about him in the epistles. And finally, there is much about him in the book of Revelation.

This being said, why does the concept of demons scare people more than the person of Satan? First, much of Christianity has been taught of the existence of Satan. There has been an acceptance of his existence as taught in Scripture. In contrast, there has been too little teaching in Christianity on the subject of demons.

The perception in the thinking of many Christians is that Satan is real but that he is a distant and an impersonal being. We know that he exists somewhere, but we do not know where. There are tens of millions of Christians worldwide, so we wonder why he would bother with us as individuals. We do know he causes some wars and natural disasters, which usually do not affect us personally.

Demons, however, are another matter. They can be around us; they may even be in us. This can cause deep concern. The answer is to draw strength from God to be victorious over any force of darkness. Jesus was victorious over Satan himself and over every demon He encountered. In Him we, too, can have victory. Instead of living in denial and fear, we can live in reality and be victorious.

Let me get a little more personal with this question? Do you fear the forces of evil? I do not speak of persons who may be evil. I speak of spiritual forces of evil. What are some of your options if you fear these forces?

You can yield to them. They tempt you. They tell you terrible things about yourself. They steal your happiness. In a sense, you can agree with these personalities of darkness. They have plans for you; but believe me, they are not good plans! By not resisting these beings you yield to them. That is exactly what they want. It is my opinion that they have a glee about themselves when they are able to wreck your life and, therefore, wreck the lives of your family members, friends, or people in your church.

You can retreat from these forces. You can delay your resistance to them. You can live in denial of their existence by always promising yourself that you will do something about the bondage in your life at some more convenient time. You can lose yourself in busywork, convincing yourself that even if all of this is true, it applies to other people—not you.

Another option is to *draw strength from the Lord for victory.* This victory does not always come easy, but it is the only path that leads to a great conclusion at the end of the journey.

IS CONFESSION A PREREQUISITE FOR DELIVERANCE?

I have been asked about the role of confession in the deliverance process. I am very familiar with James 5:15-16 (NIV) where the Scripture says, *"If they have sinned, they will be forgiven. Therefore confess your sins to each other and pray for each other so that you may be healed."*

I believe there are times when the Holy Spirit calls upon a person to confess his or her sins to an individual or to a group. I have witnessed a pastor stand before the entire congregation and confess sexual sins. (I must say that it was painful to watch.) I have witnessed another pastor stand before a presbytery and confess the sin of shoplifting. I have been with a group of church leaders and heard a father confess his sexual sins against his daughters who were present. The list could go on and on.

From years of experience of casting demons out of people, I find a general, even private, confession of sin is very helpful. I don't find it necessary to have a lengthy period of time confessing individual sins to those preparing to minister deliverance.

Am I minimizing the need for repentance when a person has wronged others? No. It may be very necessary and God-honoring for such a person to repent.

If someone ministering deliverance requires confession of sin before deliverance happens, I would say that is his or her approach to deliverance. If it works for them, that is fine. To my knowledge, there is no biblical reference that says it is a prerequisite to the deliverance process. It may be necessary to cast out the demons that drove the person into sin in the first place before that person can even recognize the depths of destruction his or her sins have caused others. At that point, confession and repentance of sin is valuable and even necessary.

WHAT ABOUT MENTAL ILLNESS?

Mental illness cannot be cast out. But, there may be demons present that agitate and inflame the mental illness. These can be cast out. At times these invading beings can cause mental illness to be almost unbearable. When these demons that compounded the mental illness are cast out, the mental illness can be more effectually treated.

Sometimes the work of demons is misdiagnosed by professionals and given the name of a mental illness. The professional can only say what science has taught them. But if the problem is purely demonic, the person can be healed by the demons being cast out.

Therefore, I very much believe that mental illnesses exist. I also believe that demons can mimic mental illness. A person might have all the symptoms of a mental illness, but in reality the symptoms are caused by demons. In this case, the demons can be cast out, and the person would be free.

In other cases where a mental illness is the correct diagnosis, the person can be helped as demons that compound mental illness are removed. In some rare cases, the ministry of deliverance can remove the symptoms that would cause a person to be correctly diagnosed as mentally ill.

The answer for correctly diagnosed mental illness is to pray for healing for that person with the mental illness. I know God heals physical illnesses. Therefore, I know God can heal mental illness. So pray for the person with mental illness to be healed!

In ministering to people who struggle in these areas, I try to be both very encouraging and also honest. I don't want to promise more than God ordinarily produces. Even when wondrous things happen, God often works through a process. God works over a period of time rather than just an impacting moment to bring healing and restoration.

IS THE MINISTRY OF DELIVERANCE ALWAYS EFFECTIVE?

Someone can sit under the best teacher in this city or attend the most anointed worship service, but it comes down to what that person does with these experiences that makes a difference in his or her future. So it is with deliverance; like any other ministry, it is what a person does with it going forward that counts.

A second part of the answer to why ministry is sometimes not completely effective is the presence of mental and emotional problems. When you cast spirits out of an emotionally or mentally struggling person, spirits that have gained entrance due to emotional weaknesses or mental incapacities will be gone, but the emotional and mental struggles still need to be addressed, as I have previously stated. Otherwise, an open door or breach still remains for demonic activity. On the other hand, if you provide for a person's mental and emotional handicaps but do not drive out the spirits, you still have problems.

The point I am attempting to make is that many people have two volcanoes erupting inside: one is caused by demons; the other is caused by emotional or mental anguish. Often we stop the lava flow from one of the volcanoes while the other volcano is still spewing.

Christianity, at least in Western Europe and North America, is much stronger in aiding the mental and emotional wounds of fellow believers. Other parts of Christianity accomplish more effective ministry with the demonic bondages. I believe that we in the West need to have the courage and determination to learn and practice spiritual warfare, while other parts of the world need to excel more in helping the emotionally wounded.

You may be wondering how all of this plays out in my ministry. With the training I received in undergraduate studies and in seminary, plus forty-seven years in the ministry, I can and sometimes do counsel people. But many times I recommend that people see a professional Christian counselor. Frankly, the counselor may do a better job than I would do. I recommend that they take the insights I discerned and share them with the counselor. The counselor may know very little or nothing about the ministry of deliverance, but the insights the Lord has given me can be a great asset in helping the counselor know the client better.

DO MINISTERS OF DELIVERANCE FULLY COMPREHEND IT?

Some who have received ministry may consider us who have ministered deliverance over a long period of time "professionals." In reality, we have only a partial knowledge of what is really going on inside the person receiving deliverance. Just as it is difficult to explain fully what happens inwardly to someone who has come to faith in the Lord Jesus Christ, it is also difficult to comprehend the inner workings of deliverance.

A person who comes to faith in Christ is a new creature. Old things have passed away and the individual is *"being transformed"* from *"glory to glory"* (2 Corinthians 3:18 NKJV). But how? So much of the answer lies in the word "faith." It is a holy mystery. While a strong case can be made from Scripture for the ministry of deliverance, we have only a limited knowledge of the inward process.

This can simply be illustrated by the following analogy. I am using a computer. I can function somewhat effectively with the computer. It is essential to the production of this book. That said, I couldn't begin to understand the inner workings of the computer. Not being able to fully comprehend the way a computer works does not keep me from putting letters on a page that, in turn, form words, which form sentences.

QUESTIONS TO CONSIDER

1. Which of these questions would you have asked if you had had the opportunity to do so?

2. What do you think would hinder a person who had demons from receiving deliverance?

3. Why do you think that the subject of demons frightens people more than the subject of Satan?

PRAYER

Dear Father, thank You for being patient with me as I seek to learn these truths, which, for the most part, are new to me. Search my heart and life. If there is anything of darkness in me, I want it gone. In Jesus' name, amen.

And, in the name of Jesus, I command any unholy spirit within me or around me to be gone. You cannot stay. I do not want you nor welcome you. The blood of the Lamb covers me. I rebuke you in the name of Jesus. You have no place in me. Be gone! Fill me, Jesus, with Your Holy Spirit. Cleanse and wash me. Thank You, Father.

Chapter Nine

CALLED TO MINISTER DELIVERANCE?

The God of peace will soon crush Satan under your feet. The grace of our Lord Jesus be with you (Romans 16:20).

I am including this chapter in the book because you may be feeling that God has given you the spiritual gift of discernment of spirits and is calling you to minister to others outside of your family. My hope is that you have seen the value of deliverance and are considering how you might learn to do this ministry.

Of course, the primary resources are the passages of the Bible that speak to spiritual warfare and the casting out of demons. The truths in these passages are the essentials. While the importance of this ministry is expressed on the pages of Scripture, there are not many practical details on how to do this ministry. So what are you to do?

If possible, find a mentor who will teach you the basics of this ministry. Part of the value of this mentor is that he or she will share practical truths with you. As you interact with the mentor, come with your questions. Write the questions out ahead of time, and if other questions come to your mind, don't hesitate to ask them. As I mentor seminary students, many times they have a notebook and are writing down my insights. This is an excellent idea.

Hopefully, the mentor will invite you to sit in on deliverance sessions where he or she is ministering. When I do this, I not only invite a student to see the reality of the ministry, but I want the student to participate in the ministry. If the student thinks a particular spirit is in the person receiving help, I will instruct that student to tell it to leave; I agree with the student in commanding out the spirit.

If time permits, ask questions of the mentor when the session is completed. Measure the mentor's style and results in light of what you have seen in Scripture. With the mentor, you are not the critic but the one there to learn. Still it is good to ask yourself how you might have done things differently, or how you could improve upon what you have learned.

Make the ministry your ministry. Blend it into your personality. Do the ministry with excellence. Above all, the most important thing you can learn from a mentor is that with Christ's help you can cast out spirits. Then, having learned it, do it!

Your gifting and your calling direct you to be involved in spiritual warfare. Be faithful to this commission. But, in turn, I also encourage you to be "a well-rounded Christian." Be a faithful attendee of a Christ-centered church. Be involved in the life of the church. I encourage you to have Christian friends and to interact with them. Hopefully, some of them will understand your ministry and support it with prayer and interest. Don't be a "lone wolf" kind of Christian. We need each other.

Some who minister in deliverance have been criticized as "seeing a demon under every rock." It is possible to blame everything on demons when only some things are caused by demons. As a person matures in this ministry, he or she is better able to discern what is caused by a demon versus what is a needed lifestyle change. Or, as I have addressed before, the problem could be strictly mental, physical, or due to sin in the person's life.

As people around us see a consistent Christian walk with the Lord, they can more easily receive from us the ministry of deliverance. They know we are committed to the Lord Jesus Christ. They observe that we sincerely try to serve Him. They know they can trust us. As I have interacted with many people over the decades who have been in this ministry, most of them have been well-balanced, thinking, considerate Christian people.

If you are a person who sees the biblical value of the ministry of deliverance, ask your pastor to preach a sermon occasionally on the subject. Encourage your small group or your Sunday school class to do a series on what the Scripture says about spiritual warfare. Because youth are so vulnerable to the destruction of darkness, suggest that a speaker be invited to do a series of meetings on the subject. College and university students would find this to be a valuable addition to their knowledge of the Lord. Husbands and wives could use this in a devotional study. Children or grandchildren could gently be introduced to spiritual warfare.

Books on the subject could be purchased and given to strategic people. In turn, the Holy Spirit might use these books to change the direction of a person's life. I encourage you to be open to the leading of the Lord for opportunities to introduce this much-needed truth into your conversations with others. I have to believe that God wants us to know about these truths because there is so much material in Scripture about the subject of spiritual warfare.

We who have embraced the reality of this ministry need to pass it on to others. One of the themes that runs throughout this book is that there are not enough responsible people in churches and in ministries who are equipped in this area of service. There is no better way to be equipped than to spend time with a capable mentor. As you learn the ministry of deliverance, consider mentoring someone else in it.

It is becoming increasingly more difficult to deny the reality of demonic activity in our culture and even in the lives of people around us. Endless are the times I have Christians speak to me concerning their loved ones. I have heard so many painful stories as people share how they have seen a totally different personality take over their loved one. When they see a different set of eyes looking out of their eyes, they know they're not dealing with their loved one but with a personality inside that loved one.

I am convinced that the Lord Jesus has given His authority to the church to see people like these set free. My greatest desire in writing this book is to move you to do something to bring freedom from spiritual bondages to your family and to any others the Lord may bring your way. One of my themes over the forty years of being a pastor was to exhort people, "Don't only be hearers of the word, but be doers of the word!" (See James 1:22.)

WHO CAN MINISTER DELIVERANCE?

Who is qualified to minister in the area of deliverance? In one sense, it is one of the gifts given to all believers. It is one of those "signs" promised to those who trust in Jesus. That being said, what are some qualities a person should have who desires or feels called to minister deliverance?

That person should recognize that deliverance is possible only as the presence of the Holy Spirit applies the accomplished work of the Lord. The person ministering should have the faith to follow wherever the Holy Spirit leads. He or she should possess a genuine compassion for the person receiving ministry. There should be a strong desire and tenaciousness to see darkness defeated. Deliverance ministers must minister out of humility, giving all the credit to the Lord Jesus and taking no credit themselves. They should be persons of prayer and steeped in the Word of God.

These personal qualities are advantageous for someone who ministers deliverance, whether occasionally or on a regular basis. These are God-given traits that will allow the Holy Spirit to flow more naturally through the person who is ministering, thus bringing freedom to the captive.

You may also ask, "Can I really do deliverance?" My answer is both yes and no. No, you can't do deliverance, but the Holy Spirit ministering in the authority of Christ can do deliverance through you. It is my opinion that the Lord Jesus would use far more people in this ministry if they were willing to be participants with Him.

WILL ANYONE BELIEVE ME?

Another question you may ask, "Will anyone believe me if I talk to them about deliverance?" It is probably true that some people will not believe you. They may think you are a bit strange; a few would go as far as to think you are foolish. There will be others, though, who will take it under consideration. You have strong support from the Word of God; and possibly, you have some support from your own experience.

I find that most people are willing to give the issue serious consideration. Some will find themselves in basic agreement with you and may even seek help in the areas of their bondages. None of us enjoys being challenged and viewed as wrong. But, as we look at the New Testament, most of the main characters were challenged at various times, and history proved them to be right!

I have had occasions where people who were in strong disagreement with the concept came back and apologized, admitting we were speaking truth concerning the ministry of deliverance. The most important matter is that we represent the Lord well; He is able to bring the results that He desires.

Another question close to the previous question is, "What will people think of me?" Scripture says, a good name is to be desired more than great riches (see Proverbs 22:1). Based on this, we work to have a good reputation. But, we also speak the truth in love (Ephesians 4:15). God's truth sometimes puts us in conflict with others around us. Many people who believe in and even practice this ministry are respected by most other believers, and sometimes are even regarded highly by secular people. To see someone wonderfully set free is worth the criticism we may receive for doing what was so important in the New Testament.

WILL I ENCOUNTER RESISTANCE?

The question is often asked, "Will I encounter resistance spiritually if I begin to minister to other people in the area of deliverance?" The short answer is, "Probably so."

We think of the people who ministered in the area of deliverance as seen in Scripture. Jesus ministered in the area of deliverance. He sent the twelve disciples out to minister in this area. We see the seventy who came back and reported that even the demons were subject to them. There was an unnamed person who was casting demons out of people. One of Jesus' disciples stopped him, but Jesus rebuked the disciple for squelching the man who was ministering in His name. So we can identify at least eighty-eight people in the New Testament era—and probably there were others—who cast out spirits. Most likely forces of darkness resisted all of these who ministered in the area of deliverance.

The temptation for many is to back away from anything that might be associated with this ministry even though they believe all of the biblical revelation about demons and may even believe the accounts of ministry in this book. While there is a price to pay for participating in spiritual warfare, there is also a price to pay for ministering in other areas of the Christian faith.

The "kickbacks" that come from dark forces are mostly just nuisances and hindrances—the car won't start, the computer acts up, the boss is difficult for no apparent reason. These hindrances can be annoying, but they can be overcome.

As someone who has experienced a blessed life for more than four decades while participating in spiritual warfare, I can say unequivocally that the rewards of helping others are more than worth the cost. I am so grateful that the persons who sowed into me and taught me this ministry were not afraid to move into the area of deliverance.

THE SUPPORTING ROLE OF DELIVERANCE IN THE CHURCH

As I have pondered the role of deliverance in modern Christianity, I have come to the conclusion that it is not a "stand-alone ministry." I believe it is an important ministry that should be integrated into other important ministries of the Christian community for a larger kingdom purpose. Without diminishing my commitment to it as a very important ministry, I view it as supporting other ministries.

Jesus faithfully proclaimed the kingdom of God, and in doing so He healed the sick and cast out demons. There was not a season of His ministry where He only healed the sick; there was not a season in His ministry where He only cast out demons. As He moved from place to place preaching the kingdom of heaven to God's special people Israel, Jesus also cast out demons and healed the sick.

Many times the laity of the church is more convinced of the reality of spiritual warfare than are the church professionals. If you are laity, I encourage you to look for opportunities to bear witness to what you see in the Scriptures and to what you are realizing in life concerning spiritual warfare. You might accomplish this objective by teaching a Sunday school class or small life group on the subject.

In addition, if you have like-minded people who sense a call to this ministry, you could approach church leadership with the request that this group have permission to minister to people in bondage. Another good avenue is to place literature about spiritual warfare in the hands of the church staff. Probably the staff members are no better trained in the subject than I was after attending seven years of higher education in preparing for the pastoral ministry.

For those who envision themselves as missionaries and are sometimes called into dark places, this ministry could be a great asset. For those who are involved in faith-based ministries that take the gospel to communities, this ministry can be invaluable. For those whose ministries focus on the business community or the sports community or the youth, there's a place and a need for this ministry.

The ministry of deliverance is better used in support of the objectives of the leadership of the ministry, mission organization, or church rather than being the sole purpose for the existence of the organization. A better balance is maintained if deliverance is not the only reason for the existence of a group of people, but rather it is incorporated into the life of a particular ministry to set people free to accomplish the Lord's call in and through that group of people.

One of the amazing things about the understanding of spiritual warfare and the ministry of deliverance is that it can be integrated into the theology of most of Christianity. If you are Catholic, Orthodox, or Evangelical, it can be accepted. To go even further, if you are an evangelical, you can be either Reformed or Armenian, and the acceptance of the reality of this ministry does not conflict with your belief system. You can be a member of a historical local church, or you can be part of a new church plant and still accept the reality of what Scripture says about dealing with darkness.

You might accept portions of my belief system and reject other portions of it, but as you have wrestled with the concepts in this book, you have at least attempted to understand what I believe is for all Christianity.

I ask you to ponder this question: *What if I am right*? Could not the body of Christ be greatly strengthened by this ministry? Could not lost people mired in great spiritual bondage first find Jesus as Deliverer and then find Him as Savior? As most of Christianity is rethinking ways of reaching those outside of the church, could this not be an instrument the church uses to proclaim that the reality of Jesus when He walked the face of the earth is the reality of Jesus applied today?

JOIN A MINISTRY TEAM

Many evangelical churches are forming ministry teams to pray for people after a Sunday morning worship service. A group of people, under the leadership of the church, who feel a call to this ministry and have been trained could be available to minister to people who have spiritual bondages. A separate room could be designated for privacy's sake. It is important for the leadership of the church to give this group of people its support. Like every other ministry in the church, this ministry will sometimes be executed imperfectly. But, the positive results will far outweigh the negative fallout.

Who should be in this group of people ministering deliverance? Each of the team members should be emotionally stable. Those involved should not be living in sin; they should be committed to the Lord. Someone who has had experience in the ministry of deliverance should train the team.

What are some guidelines for this group of people as they minister in this unique work? I believe that there should be some kind of reporting to the church leadership of the results of the ministry. The names and the details of those who receive ministry should be kept private, but some kind of general reporting could keep the group connected with the church leadership. At least two members of the ministry team should be present anytime ministry takes place. I have seen this done successfully in a historical denominational church. A group of laypeople minister to approximately one hundred twenty people each year from inside and outside the church.

DELIVERANCE IN A GROUP SETTING

The first deliverance I saw took place in a large assembly room with five hundred people in attendance. God moved powerfully. I came out of that meeting convinced of the reality of the ministry and its value for today. The advantage of group deliverance is that more people can be touched at the same time. Also, people may not feel as conspicuous because they are not the only ones receiving ministry. The disadvantages are that some of the personal touch and thoroughness of one-on-one ministry are lost.

How does group deliverance work? The leader could begin by teaching on the subject from a biblical perspective. Then he or she could lead the group in a time of preliminary ministry by breaking generational curses and any spiritual holds that may be keeping someone bound. Next, the leader could ask the people in the silence of their hearts to forgive those who have wronged them. Again, in the silence of their hearts, they could confess sins to the Lord. The leader could ask them if they have had any occult involvement or any involvement in New Age or non-Christian religions. These involvements should be repented of and renounced.

After these steps, the leader can begin to call out the inner impressions being receiving from the Lord. A number of people may be struggling with the same spirit. The leader may say, "Search your heart to know if this is you who have that spirit. If so, agree with the Lord that He will drive it out. If you do not have that particular spirit, then intercede for the person or persons who do need the Lord to cast the spirit out."

As I do this ministry, at some point I will encourage the group to hear from the Holy Spirit. If the Holy Spirit shows them other spirits that should be cast out, then I ask them to name that spirit and I will tell it to leave. After this has happened, I go a step further. The next person who has an impression from the Holy Spirit of a demon that is present, I have them cast it out. What has happened is that people who have never seen deliverance are not only seeing it, but are actually being used of God to cause it to happen.

Did Jesus ever do group deliverance? My best guess is that He did not. With His level of anointing, everything might have been bedlam had He done so. With my level of anointing it is very orderly. Also, I expect that the people who encountered Jesus were in far more desperate shape than are most of the people to whom I minister.

Group ministry can be effective with five people or with a thousand people. People leave knowing that God has been at work. Something has happened. People often approach me and tell me what God did for them during the ministry time. I then close the group ministry session on a positive note by praying that the Holy Spirit will fill areas in their hearts where spirits have been cast out. Concluding the ministry with the group, I make myself available to do one-on-one ministry with individuals who may need special attention. If there are other experienced men or women who have been used of God in this ministry, I will ask them to join me in order that more people may receive ministry.

THE DELIVERANCE MINISTRY FUTURE

As I look forward, I often ponder what is ahead for the deliverance ministry. What is on the Lord's heart? Let me begin with what I believe to be on God's timetable. I believe we are going to see a mighty move of God in the world. People who are now living very dark and broken lives will come to faith. Some of these will come out of established world religious systems such as Islam. Leading this movement will be youth and young adults. They will come with total commitment to faith in Jesus, but many will continue to struggle with great spiritual bondages in their lives.

Therefore, on one hand there will be a radical commitment to Jesus Christ as Lord and Savior, and on the other hand there will be spiritual bondages that will hamper their effectiveness. My desire and prayer—and I believe the Lord's heart—is that the worldwide church would have many people trained to set the captives free.

Some of what I predict is already happening. But, I believe it is only the beginnings of what God will yet do! Am I trying to say one size fits all, that deliverance is the solution to all the problems of all these people? No, what I propose is only part of the picture, but it *is* part of it.

I am being approached by an increasing number of teenagers and young adults who are seeking ministry. They have been involved in all kinds of sin. Some have come from broken homes and broken situations. They have been living in Sodom and Gomorrah rather than in the Promised Land. But their hearts are to serve the Lord, and His heart is for them to serve Him. They well could be the answer to the prayers that many of us prayed for years, yes, even for decades. We need to give them every possibility to succeed! I know something is happening in this culture, and by faith I believe it will increase greatly.

I predict that the ministry of deliverance will be more widely accepted by people in secular society, as well as in the church. As more people share their stories with acquaintances and family concerning the impact that this ministry has had in their lives, people will become more open to its concepts.

Shifting gears and along the same lines, I would like to encourage you to read one book a year on the subject of spiritual warfare. There are numerous books on the market that would be informative. There is a growing interest in congregations to be informed about spiritual warfare as the increase of evil throughout the world is heralded in the media. You may or may not agree with every author's position and experiences, but exposure to these books would keep the reality of spiritual warfare before you. In addition, it would help you find your place in this battle. I am convinced that as Jesus came to tread the works of Satan underfoot, we each have a responsibility in this ongoing work.

ACTION WORDS

As we minister deliverance, there are a lot of words spoken. There are words, and then there are *action* words. The action words accomplish the purposes of the Lord. What do I mean by this? Sometimes, the person or persons ministering deliverance find themselves speaking a lot about deliverance and about the needs of the person receiving the ministry rather than using action words to order the spiritual bondage in the person to be gone. The same can be said for the person receiving the ministry.

Recently a pastor sent one of his parishioners to my wife and me to receive ministry. As we met with her, it became obvious that the lady was more interested in talking and finding someone to agree with her destructive lifestyle than to free her of spiritual bondages.

In this ministry we can simply become one more person listening to a troubled person's problems. Or we can bring the individual or a group of people to the place where they are willing to be prayed for to receive freedom from what occupies them and holds them in bondage. Do I believe in listening to people's pains and conflicts? Yes, and I have done much of that over the years. But to defeat Satan's hold on a person's being, there must be commands, action words, to drive away the beings that have created havoc and bondage in that person.

I usually use a number of words to describe this ministry to individuals who are seeking help. But from many years of experience I have come to know that if the

Lord is going to make a real difference in their lives, the authority of the Lord Jesus Christ must be applied. Someone *must* command demonic beings to leave. This is done politely and with respect for the person, but freedom comes when action words are spoken to the spirits.

For most of us in this busy world, the time that we can give to an individual is limited. Therefore we need to make wise use of the limited time we can invest in someone. There are other people God has gifted to be the primary listeners to those who deeply need to share their innermost thoughts. I hope your special contribution will be to use action words, letting Jesus be your example, to drive darkness from the person.

THE PIECES OF THE PUZZLE

Most people have worked on puzzles. For some, it was something done as a child or as a youth. For others, putting puzzles together is a lifetime hobby. Recently my wife bought a 1,000-piece puzzle for our grandchildren to put together on a beach vacation. The beach was too much competition, and the puzzle did not get completed—maybe next year.

Think with me of obtaining a puzzle with a lovely scene unfolding before your eyes as you join piece after piece. As you begin to reach the completion of the puzzle, you realize that some pieces are missing. Disappointment crashes into your world. Part of the picture is missing; it is not complete.

This story is an illustration of the church trying to instruct its people to walk the Christian walk without the benefit of all the truths and the effects of those truths God means for us to have. We need these truths and our precious people need these truths to defeat the spiritual enemy that wants to defeat the church of the living God. I encourage you to be an instrument in the Lord's hand to supply the missing puzzle pieces.

A CALL TO RETURN TO MINISTRY

Much of the focus of this book has been to instruct and encourage the individual and families concerning dealing with spiritual bondages based on Scripture, as well as to underline scriptural principles with personal experience. Recently I said to several people, "We could easily use a thousand more people skilled in this ministry right here in this city where we live." The answer came back from a friend who is in full-time ministry, "That's true!"

Because of the pressing need for more people to minister deliverance than are currently available, I would like to speak to those who have ministered in this way in the past, but for whatever reason do not minister in the present.

I understand why a person may not continue to pursue this ministry. Even our fellow Christians often misunderstand those of us who minister. There are those who do not fully comprehend what we are doing or why we are doing it. Also, there is a real price to pay because of increased attacks from Satan's forces who want to stop our efforts.

You may have dropped out because you feel like you have erred at times. All of us who have ministered in spiritual warfare have at times made mistakes. On the other hand, some of the people we have invested ourselves in did not choose to walk out their deliverance coupled with a disciplined Christian lifestyle. Consequently, it appeared that our ministry had been in vain because of their destructive choices.

There are others who are equipped and gifted to minister deliverance, but the cares and burdens of a busy lifestyle have sidetracked you from helping a needy person in bondage. It was not an intentional decision; it just happened.

If you are one of the persons I have described, I encourage you to take the necessary steps to return to the ministry to which God has called you. It might involve making some sacrifices, but it can make a real difference in lives that receive and respond to your ministry. It is like riding a bicycle; you never really forget how to ride it. If you will take that step to return to this ministry, the how-to will return. And someone held captive will experience freedom.

QUESTIONS TO CONSIDER

1. What steps going forward might you take to increase your understanding of deliverance?

2. How might you encourage those in your church to consider more seriously their involvement in spiritual warfare as a ministry?

3. What effect(s) has this book had on your understanding of deliverance?

4. How will you use the instruction in this training manual to minister to your children or to others?

PRAYER

Oh, Holy Spirit, come and fill me up that I might be Your instrument to accomplish all You have called me to do. Continue to instruct me in Your ways and in Your truths. May I walk with wisdom and discernment. May *"Thy kingdom come and Thy will be done here on earth as it is in heaven!"* With praise and worship to the Lord of lords and King of kings! Amen.

Chapter Ten

A JOURNEY THROUGH THE SCRIPTURES

Finally, be strong in the Lord and in the strength of His might. Stand firm, therefore, having girded your loins with truth…in addition to all, taking up the shield of faith with which you will be able to extinguish all the flaming arrows of the evil one. And take…the sword of the Spirit, which is the word of God (Ephesians 6:10,14,16-17).

Although I have relied on Scripture throughout this book, we will now go on a somewhat abbreviated journey through the Scripture to underline the importance of spiritual warfare in our Christian walk. You may be surprised how often the biblical writers address the subject. It is important to know and understand what the Word of God says about Satan and the demonic and about the power and authority given to the believer by the Lord Jesus Christ.

THE OLD TESTAMENT

We will begin by looking at the book of Deuteronomy. In Deuteronomy 18:9-14, we hear these sobering words from God, *"When you enter the land which the Lord*

179

your God gives you, you shall not learn to imitate the detestable things of those nations." The Jewish people are instructed not to behave according to the abominable practices of the nations they are dispossessing. Deuteronomy 18:12 states, *"because of these detestable things the Lord your God will drive them out before you."*

What was Israel not to do that the Canaanites were doing?

> *Let no one be found among you who sacrifices his son or his daughter in the fire, who practices divination or sorcery, interprets omens, engages in witchcraft, or casts spells, or who is a medium or spiritist or who consults the dead* (Deuteronomy 18:10-11 NIV).

This passage has a way of speaking soberly to people who do not ordinarily give attention to the supernatural. Persons who would not give much attention to spiritual warfare see how seriously God takes the occult and its destructiveness. They may even remember times they have dabbled in the occult. In the Scripture passage we have just looked at, nations are dispossessed because of total involvement in what is an offense to the living God.

Let us look at another passage. In the Old Testament, the Holy Spirit came upon persons to accomplish the purposes of God. In First Samuel 16:14-23 we learn that Saul, the first king of Israel, experienced the departure of the Holy Spirit due to his disobedience. Then an evil spirit came upon him. Even Saul's attendants recognized it to be an evil spirit. This was a thousand years before Christ. The unnamed servants were more perceptive than most people in our churches today. Recognizing Saul's tormented dilemma, they tried to help him by bringing in David to play his anointed music for the king. The evil spirit would leave the king, at least for a season.

The end results of these efforts were not great. In First Samuel 18:10-11 we see an evil spirit coming forcefully upon Saul. Saul, with a spear in his hand, hurled it at David saying, *"I will pin David to the wall."* Here we see an evil spirit of destruction that would have driven Saul to destroy the man who was faithful to him and who was destined to be Israel's greatest king. Saul's hatred of David, intensified by a spirit of destruction, caused the perfect storm. If the spirit had prevailed, it would have destroyed the very person who was helping Saul, and who would later greatly help the nation of Israel, and from whose lineage would come our precious Lord Jesus.

This event is repeated in First Samuel 19:9-13. Again, it was an evil spirit that came upon Saul. Both the spirit and Saul wanted to destroy David. Finally, and wisely, David followed his wife's advice and fled for his life.

In First Kings 22:15 we see the prophet Micaiah prophesying to a combined army of Israel and Judah. He speaks of a vision the Lord had shown him. Micaiah said, *"…I saw the Lord sitting on His throne with all the host of heaven standing by Him on His right and on His left"* (1 Kings 22:19). What a scene! Can we not agree this was an awesome picture? But the scene continues.

God in His justice would destroy the wicked king of Israel. He asked the host of heaven how this would be accomplished. In First Kings 22:21-22 (NIV), a spirit comes forward to suggest, *"'I will entice him.' 'By what means?' the Lord asked. 'I will go out and be a deceiving spirit in the mouths of all his prophets.'"*

Because these were false prophets, it was easy for heaven to allow the request to become reality. The Lord's answer to the spirit was, *"Go and do it."* We see God's sovereignty and just will being accomplished. God is taking very seriously Israel's gross sins. The particular spirit that proposed this solution took to itself the nature of a deceiving or lying spirit.

Lying spirits still function today. They cause people to verbalize untruths. Another function of a lying spirit is to lie to the person they inhabit, thus causing that person to believe things about themselves or about others that are false. Often the person is like the false prophets in Scripture; they want to believe a lie and to speak a lie for their own personal gain.

Returning to the story in First Kings 22 about Micaiah's vision, we see the false prophets declaring a great victory for Ahab. But just the opposite unfolded; the combined armies of Israel and Judah were defeated, and wicked King Ahab was killed in the conflict.

In Second Kings 19:5-7 we see another incident in the Old Testament concerning spirits. The great prophet Isaiah spoke to Hezekiah, the king of Judah. Because the king of the feared Assyrian nation was moving an army toward Jerusalem, Hezekiah was terribly frightened. Isaiah, speaking for God, said of the king of Assyria, *"Behold, I will put a spirit in him so that he will hear a rumor and return to his own land; and I will cause him to fall by the sword in his own land."* Isaiah, the speaker of some of the greatest words in the Old Testament, informs us that spirits not only exist but can cause deception and affect the affairs of people.

Many scholars believe that Job was the first book of the Bible to be put into writing. In Job 4:15-16 (NIV) we see these words: *"A spirit glided past my face and the hair on my body stood on end. It stopped, but I could not tell what it was. A form stood before my eyes, and I heard a hushed voice."* In some of the earliest writings in Scripture we see the existence of spiritual beings. Some of these are evil and some of these are good, but they did exist. They exist today, and they affect the affairs of people in the twenty-first century!

Now we look at the prophet Hosea who is prophesying against Israel. In Hosea 4:12 (NIV) he says of Israel: *"My people consult a wooden idol, and a diviner's rod speaks to them. A spirit of prostitution leads them astray...."* Here it is not clear whether this is an attitude of prostitution or a literal spirit of prostitution that was leading them astray. From forty-seven years of experience battling in spiritual warfare, I would say it could be as easily a spirit of prostitution as it would be a base human desire. Probably it was both.

Some people see the events described in the material we have viewed as fanciful pictures or illustrations from human imaginations. The writers knew these events to be real and the beings described to exist. With the Old Testament writers I see them as literal beings. These beings could cause a group of false prophets to lie. An evil spirit could cause Saul to hurl a spear at David. A spirit could appear to Job and cause his hair to stand on end. A spirit, described by Isaiah as a deceiving spirit, could deceive a pagan king and cause his destruction.

All these concepts are not clearly defined and developed. Yet, we see spiritual beings called spirits introduced in the writings of the Old Testament. As we view these biblical passages we have more questions than we have answers. What we do know is that spiritual beings existed and do exist. They affected human behavior. These spiritual beings affect human behavior today. One of these beings defined itself as evil. Another called itself a deceiving or lying spirit.

As we look into the ministry of Christ and the ministry of many other personalities in the New Testament, we have far more insight into the spiritual world. Spiritual warfare would be a primary ministry in their lives. So now we direct our attention to their ministries in order to increase our knowledge about spiritual beings. This understanding can greatly enhance the concept of freedom in our lives. These truths may be the key to help family members and friends who struggle with oppression.

THE GOSPELS

Matthew

In Matthew 4 we see the personal encounter of the Lord Jesus with Satan. While there is much to be learned from this passage, I want to emphasize one point. We see two real personalities in the conflict. We see the Son of God who was just beginning His formal ministry. Also, we see Satan. As Jesus is a real being, Satan is a real being. He was not a symbolic, imaginary representative of evil. In the encounter with Jesus, he is perceptible. Many areas of Christianity believe he was an outstanding angel who led a revolt against God and, along with a host of other angels, was cast out of heaven.

Satan opposed Jesus. Jesus resisted him and dealt with Satan as a real personality. Each time Satan challenged Jesus, Jesus answered him with portions of Scripture. Here were two beings in conflict, one perfectly holy and one perfectly evil. They both existed; Jesus was not talking to Himself! This encounter ended with Satan leaving and angels coming to minister to Jesus.

At the end of chapter 4, Matthew wrote the following:

> *Jesus went throughout Galilee, teaching in their synagogues, preaching the good news of the kingdom, and healing every disease and sickness…people brought to him all who were ill with various diseases, who suffered severe pain, the demon-possessed, those having seizures, and the paralyzed; and he healed them* (Matthew 4:23-24 NIV).

In the modern church it is important for believers to recognize that Jesus' primary ministries were to preach the good news of the kingdom, to cast out demons, and to heal the sick.

Just before recording the Sermon on the Mount, Matthew tells us about Jesus' ministry of casting out demons. It is of special importance to remind ourselves that Jesus was ministering to God's chosen ones. He was ministering to the Jewish people who gave us the Old Testament and even the Messiah Himself. In their heritage were Isaiah, David, Deborah, and Esther. Yet, Jesus saw the pressing need to minister deliverance to many of them.

In the Sermon on the Mount, we find the prayer the Lord taught His disciples. Often it is called the Lord's Prayer. In the last verse of this prayer we find the words,

"Lead us not into temptation, but deliver us from the evil one" (Matthew 6:13 NIV). Some Bible translations word this as *"deliver us from evil."* In many churches this prayer is prayed every Sunday without the congregation giving much thought to the words—but in the prayer the Lord actually taught His followers to ask to be delivered from the evil one.

Since Satan is not omnipresent, there are spiritual forces throughout the world that represent him. Without realizing it, many who pray this prayer are asking the Lord to free them from the bondages that are in their lives. They may also be asking, without realizing it, for the Lord to protect them from future bondage. This prayer takes on even more meaning when the individual or the congregation praying the prayer realizes the Lord wants to protect them from forces of darkness. It would be helpful for church leaders to call this insight to the attention of their congregations. This prayer and, thus, this teaching moment, came from the lips of Jesus.

In Matthew 8, we see Jesus coming into Peter's home. Peter's mother-in-law is lying in bed with a fever; Jesus touches her hand, and she is healed. When evening comes, the Scripture says that many who were demon-possessed were brought to Jesus, and He drove out the spirits with a word and healed all the sick. Matthew continues by stating this event occurred to fulfill what was spoken to the prophet Isaiah, *"...He Himself took our infirmities and carried away our diseases"* (Matthew 8:17). The Lord Jesus Christ powerfully ministered to precious people by bringing healing to them *and* by casting demons out of many.

In Matthew 9, we see a man brought to Jesus. This man was demon-possessed and could not speak. When the demon was driven out, the man who had been mute now spoke. The crowd was amazed and declared, *"Nothing like this has ever been seen in Israel"* (Matthew 9:33).

One of the most convincing verses in Scripture concerning the ministry of deliverance is found in Matthew 12:28 (NIV). Matthew wrote, quoting Jesus, *"If it is by the Spirit of God that I drive out demons, then the kingdom of God has come upon you."* It appears from this verse that Jesus is defining His kingdom by saying that driving out demons authenticates who He is. It amazes me that one of the authenticating truths of the New Testament concerning Jesus is rarely presented in our teachings. Jesus declared that because He cast out demons, we can know God's kingdom is here. That demonstrates how significant the ministry of deliverance is! The Scripture declares that the Lord is the same yesterday, today, yes, and forever. If it was true in Jesus' day, then it is equally true in our day.

In Matthew 15, we see that Jesus withdrew to the region of Tyre and Sidon. A Canaanite woman approaches Him and cries out to Him that her daughter is suffering terribly from demon possession. After a fairly lengthy conversation, Jesus commends her for her great faith! Her request is granted, and He heals her daughter. This is the only recorded time that a non-Jewish person received deliverance from the Lord Jesus. Again, it makes the point that His ministry was focused on the house of Israel, His own people. If this was true in Jesus' day, it is true in our day when oftentimes even the redeemed need this ministry!

In Matthew 16:19 (NIV), Jesus says, *"I will give you the keys of the kingdom of heaven; whatever you bind on earth will be bound in heaven, and whatever you loose on earth will be loosed in heaven."* We see authority being given by the Lord Jesus Christ to His followers. It is the authority to bind and loose, to drive out, and to pray into the people who are very needy spiritually.

One of the most dramatic scenes in the Gospels is the time the Lord Jesus went up with Peter, James, and John on what is called the Mount of Transfiguration. Two figures from the past, Moses and Elijah, appear to Jesus. After this literal mountaintop experience, the Lord comes down from the mountain; there is a man waiting whose situation is desperate. He cries out to Jesus, *"Lord, have mercy on my son...I brought him to your disciples, but they could not heal him"* (Matthew 17:15-16 NIV). We would assume that Jesus would be very understanding toward His disciples who could not heal the man's son, but He instead called them an *"unbelieving and perverse generation"* (Matthew 17:17 NIV).

Then we see Jesus rebuke the demon that comes out of the boy. He was healed from that moment. The disciples, chastened by the event, question Jesus as to why they could not cast out the demon. He replies, *"Because you have so little faith..."* (Matthew 17:20 NIV). He goes on to say that if they had the faith, then nothing would be impossible for them. In this incidence, we see the great value of faith coupled with taking authority over darkness; thus, precious people are set free.

In Matthew 18:19 (NIV) Jesus states, *"If two of you on earth agree about anything they ask for, it will be done by my Father in heaven."* I am reminded of another scriptural promise that states that where two or three gather together in His name, there He is with them (see Matthew 18:20). We see two great promises here of the power of agreement. If another person or persons is in agreement with us in ministry, we have added authority. Most importantly, there is the promise that by the work of His Holy Spirit, Jesus is present where two or three of us come together in His name.

In Matthew 21:12-13, we see the account of Jesus entering the temple area and driving out all who were buying and selling there. As He overturned the tables of the money changers, He said, *"It is written, 'My house shall be called a house of prayer'; but you are making it a robbers' den."* Here is an analogy of a deep spiritual truth. Jesus drives out the corrupt from the temple; in the spiritual realm He drove out the corrupting influences from people. Just as the temple was a special place for the presence of God to dwell, Scripture teaches that we are temples of the Holy Spirit. Just as corrupting influences existed in the most holy place of all, so corrupting spirits can dwell in the holy place of righteous persons.

Mark

We are inclined to think of the subject of deliverance as a subject for the spiritually mature. The gospel writer Mark quickly disproves this. In the first chapter of Mark there are two major references to Jesus ministering deliverance. In Mark 1:21-26 (NIV), Jesus enters a synagogue in Capernaum and begins to teach. In the synagogue there was a man who had an evil spirit. This man cries out, *"What do you want with us, Jesus of Nazareth? Have you come to destroy us? I know who you are—the Holy One of God!"* Jesus speaks sternly to the demon to be quiet and then commands it to come out of the man. The evil spirit violently shook the poor man and came out with a shriek.

After this event, Mark states that news of Jesus spread quickly over the entire region of Galilee. We have no record that anything like this event ever happened in the Old Testament. Therefore, we have portrayed in this ministry snapshot one of the major marks of the work of God in the New Testament. Remember, this man was in the synagogue; Jesus was ministering to God's chosen people. I believe the demons used these titles for Jesus to show off their insight and to say in essence, "Don't interrupt my occupying and torment. This person is mine."

As we continue in Mark 1, Jesus then goes to the home of Simon whose mother-in-law was in bed with a fever. Jesus heals her, and she immediately gets up and begins to wait on Him and the disciples. That evening people brought to Jesus all the sick and those who were troubled by demons. The whole town gathered at the door of Peter's home, and Jesus healed many who had various diseases. He also drove out many demons, but He would not let the demons speak because they knew who He was. Capernaum was a deeply religious community; archaeologists have found the remains of four synagogues there. Yet, it is evident that these people needed the powerful help that Jesus could bring to them as He healed some of them and cast demons out of others.

In Mark 3:11 we see these words, *"Whenever the unclean* [evil] *spirits saw Him, they would fall down before Him and shout, 'You are the Son of God!'"* Since evil spirits do not have physical bodies to fall down, what Mark is saying is that the demons cause those people whose bodies they had invaded to fall down. Without physical bodies of their own, demons want to use our bodies to accomplish their mischief. They wish to resist God, hurt those around us, or hurt us by their activities.

I think of demons as parasites. Having been raised in a rural area, I often heard words like hookworms, tapeworms, and ringworms. These are literal physical conditions. Demons are spiritual parasites that invade our inner person and drain life from us as did those parasites of yesteryear. People can function with those parasites, but who would want to?

In Mark 3:13, we see Jesus going up on a mountainside and calling to Himself those He wanted to be His disciples. He appointed twelve men, designating them apostles, to be with Him and to send them out to preach and have authority to drive out demons. The apostles' authority to cast out demons came from Jesus. This was also true with the seventy whom Jesus sends out later. (We will look at this event in the section on the book of Luke.)

We, too, have authority to cast out demons. Our authority comes from the accomplished work of the Lord Jesus Christ. The disciples' authority came from association with the Lord and the call He had upon their lives. The realization that the Lord Jesus gave the apostles and others the authority to command spiritual beings to leave—and they left—catches our attention. To know that we also have this authority in the twenty-first century is spectacular!

In Mark 3:22, Jesus' enemies accused Him of driving out demons by the prince of demons. Instead of attributing the work of deliverance to the Holy Spirit, they attributed it to Beelzebub. It is important to note that these detractors did not deny that Jesus drove out the demons. Major and obvious changes had occurred in the people who were receiving His ministry; therefore, it was impossible for them to say the ministry did not work.

Those in opposition to Jesus attributed the casting out of demons to darkness rather than to the work of God in their midst. Can you imagine these people standing before the judgment seat of God having said that the Son of God was possessed by Beelzebub and that He drove out demons by the prince of demons?! There are people today who border on the same kind of blasphemy, who also may have to stand before God and explain why they attributed the work of the Holy Spirit to darkness!

In the fifth chapter of Mark, the apostles spend twenty verses relating the story of Jesus healing the demon-possessed man. This pitiful man lived among the tombs and could not even be chained down because he tore the chains apart. No one was strong enough to subdue him. He would cry out and cut himself with stones. When he saw Jesus at a distance, he ran and fell on his knees in front of Him and shouted at the top of his voice, *"'What do you want with me, Jesus, Son of the Most High God?' ...For Jesus had said to him, 'Come out of this man, you impure spirit!'"* (Mark 5:7-8 NIV).

The pure love of Jesus was being poured out on this man as He gave him what he most needed—his freedom. Then Jesus asked the spirits inside the man, *"What is your name?"* The answer came back, not from the man but from the demons inside the man, *"My name is Legion...for we are many."* The demons begged Jesus not to send them out of the area but rather into a large herd of pigs nearby. Jesus gave them permission, and the evil spirits rushed out of the man and into the herd of pigs, numbering about 2,000. The pigs rushed down the steep bank and into the lake and were drowned—a picture of the power of torment! (See Mark 5:9-13.)

In contrast, a freed man sits before us on the pages of Scripture, unshackled, at peace, and of sound mind—a portrayal of the glorious, conquering, delivering power of our Savior!

One social scientist has stated that all the marks of personality are seen in this group of demons inside the tormented man:

- There was self-recognition (*"my name is Legion"*).

- There is recognition of others (they knew that Jesus was the Son of God).

- There was will (the demons begged Jesus not to send them out of the area).

- There was entreaty (*"send us among the pigs"*).

- There was movement (they move from the pitiful man into the pigs).

From this vivid account of Jesus' ministry, we can glean insight into what a demon is. It is a disembodied spirit. This simply means it is a spirit without a body. With no physical body with which to fulfill its own mischief, it chooses to enter a person and use that person to do its dastardly deeds. It doesn't like the person, or the people around the one it has entered.

What are some of the results of this powerful encounter with demons? People came from a nearby town and found the man sitting there dressed and in his right mind. This scared them terribly! How would they respond to this mighty work of God in their midst? We would expect them to plead with Jesus to come into their town and help other people, but just the opposite occurred. They pled with Jesus to leave their region. Their fear of the mighty acts of God caused them to miss the greatest blessings possible in their lives! They could have seen Jesus' miracles and heard His transforming teachings. How sad!

On the other hand, the restored man begged Jesus to let him travel with Him. Jesus answered, "Go home to your family and tell them how much the Lord has done for you and how He has had mercy on you." The man went away and began to tell the people how much Jesus had done for him; the people were amazed. I have seen this reality lived out endless times. A person would be set free by the ministry of deliverance; he would tell friends about it; the friends would then come asking for the same ministry.

As we think of the man cutting himself with stones in his torment, I cannot help but think of precious young people in our own culture today cutting their own bodies because of their torments. Is there not the same delivering power of the Lord Jesus available for them? I know there is!

One final comment on this passage. Sara Jo and I have been blessed to make many trips to Israel. (If you have not gone, I encourage you to put that on your "must-do list.") On my fourteenth trip to Israel, we were surprised to visit an area about which we knew nothing. Near the eastern shore of the Sea of Galilee there is a park named Kursi National Park. In the 1970s, a road was being built to the Golan Heights and, in doing so, a number of foundations of ancient ruins were unearthed.

Archaeologists were called in to investigate these ruins. It was determined that the ruins were from a Christian settlement built in the fifth century on the traditional site of Jesus' miracle of casting demons out of the man often called the "Gadarene demoniac." The Christian settlement had been constructed on the ancient site identified in the Talmud as Kursi, a center of idol worship.

The largest Byzantine monastery in Israel had been built there. Also, a church and a chapel were discovered there. Pilgrims from other lands traveling to see biblical Israel would travel to this site for several centuries until foreign invaders destroyed it during the ninth century.

I mention all of this to show the value that early Christianity placed on this event from the life and ministry of Jesus. The former buildings, which are now just foundation stones, are a testament to this great confrontation Jesus had with the demonic.

As we continue in the book of Mark, let us look at Mark 7:25. We see a woman coming to Jesus and falling at His feet. An evil spirit possessed her little daughter. The mother begs Jesus to drive the demon out of her daughter. As we look more closely at this passage, we notice something unique about this woman. She is a Gentile, a

Greek born in Syro-Phoenecia. As I have stated before, Jesus' main ministry was to the Jewish people, God's chosen ones. Here we see Jesus doing the unusual and ministering to a non-Jewish person.

Jesus was so powerful in His ministry against darkness that He just spoke the command, and the demon left the daughter. The mother hurries home and finds the child lying in her bed, and the demon gone. Another interesting observation in this passage is that the mother perceived her daughter to be in bondage even though the child was young. One translation calls her the "little daughter."

You may be saying that it is not fair that a spirit could invade a child. I agree. But it is reality, and it is wise to deal with reality and to minister where it is needed. The Bible tells us that Jesus taught that where two or three have gathered together in His name, He is there in the midst of them. I love to quote this verse to a child I am ministering to saying, in essence, that Jesus is here through His Spirit to minister just like He ministered when He was on earth. I will tell the child that Jesus said, *"Let the little children come to Me"* (Matthew 19:14 NKJV). He also took children in His arms and blessed them. This same Jesus can work through us and minister to precious children today.

Let us look at another passage of Scripture. In Mark 9:25 (NIV) we see Jesus rebuking an evil spirit in a young man. He referred to it as a *"deaf and mute spirit."* Jesus then commands it to *"come out of him and never enter him again."* Of importance in this brief passage is the phrase *"never enter him again."* As I minister in the area of deliverance, I often command the spirit never to enter again the person who is receiving ministry. I believe we have this authority. Certainly we have a great example in the ministry of our Lord Jesus Christ.

The disciples had not been able to drive the spirit out. It must have been an extremely strong spirit. They asked Jesus why they could not drive it away. His reply was, *"This kind comes out only by prayer";* some translations add, *"and fasting."* Strong spirits may take more earnest prayer in preparation for the ministry than what we might call "ordinary ministry" would entail. I always try to pray ahead of time if I have a ministry session scheduled. If you are called into the deliverance ministry, I encourage you to be a person of prayer. This should not be just occasionally praying, but praying on a consistent basis. Get others to join you in earnest prayer, and believe that you can drive the spirit out in the name and power of Jesus!

In Mark 16:15-17 (NIV), Jesus speaks of the Great Commission: *"Go into all the world and preach the gospel to all creation. Whoever believes and is baptized will be saved, but whoever does not believe will be condemned. And these signs will accompany those who believe: In my name they will drive out demons...."* Important in this passage is the statement, *"these signs will accompany those who believe."*

Often, as I teach spiritual warfare to a group of people, I will ask them, "Who in this room believe?" All the hands go up! So, they declare that they believe. Then I assure them that based on Scripture, they can cast out demons. This may be an occasional ministry and not a regular ministry for a Christian, but he or she can appropriate the authority and power of Christ and cast spirits out of someone as the Holy Spirit would lead them to do so!

Luke

In the first three chapters of the book of Luke, the gospel writer recounts for us the advent of the Lord Jesus Christ, as well as the birth and ministry of John the Baptist, and the genealogy of Jesus. Luke 4 begins with spiritual warfare. The Holy Spirit led the Lord Jesus into the wilderness where He encountered His archenemy Satan.

Because Jesus had been on a forty-day fast, He was in a weakened condition for this encounter. Three temptations followed. The Lord was victorious in each of these seductions although the temptations were strong and subtle. Scripture says, *"When the devil had finished all this tempting, he left Him until an opportune time"* (Luke 4:13

NIV). If Satan was audacious enough to harass the very Son of God, why are we surprised when we encounter attacks by the minions of Satan?

After this encounter, Jesus returned to His home in Nazareth and entered the synagogue as was His custom. He stood up to read from the scroll of the prophet Isaiah. In the passage that He read is this phrase, *"He has sent me to proclaim freedom for the prisoners."* After He had read the passage from Isaiah, He said to those gathered in the synagogue, *"Today this Scripture is fulfilled in your hearing"* (See Luke 4:16-21). Among the many acts of compassion that the Lord would fulfill in His years of formal ministry, He would most certainly bring freedom to the spiritually imprisoned.

Before Luke 4 ends, we see in verse 33 these words, *"In the synagogue there was a man possessed by a demon, an impure* [evil] *spirit."* Here is insight into the world of darkness. Luke equates a demon with an impure or evil spirit. We see evidence here that the words *demon, evil spirit*, and *impure, unclean spirit* are interchangeable. After Jesus cast out the demon, the people are amazed, saying to each other, *"With authority and power he gives orders to impure* [evil] *spirits and they come out!"* The Scripture continues, *"And the news about him spread throughout the surrounding area"* (see Luke 4:33-37 NIV).

Part of Jesus' reputation was formed by His authority over evil spirits. First-century people were very impressed that He had this authority. Would that twenty-first-century people be as amazed at His dominion in this area as were the first-century people!

In Luke 6:40 (NIV) the gospel writer asserts, *"The student is not above the teacher, but everyone who is fully trained will be like their teacher."* As we are seeing account after account of Jesus ministering to precious people who were in bondage to evil spirits, we hear this call from Luke to be like our Teacher, Jesus. If He boldly encountered darkness, should we not boldly confront darkness also?

In the seventh chapter of Luke, we see two disciples of John the Baptist asking Jesus if He is really the Messiah or should they look for someone else. Jesus demonstrates ten reasons why He is the long-expected One. He cured many diseases and afflictions and evil spirits; He healed the blind, the lame, the lepers, the deaf, etc. Nine of those ten reasons are what we would call grace gifts; deliverance is included in that list Jesus gave.

If Jesus defined His ministry to John's disciples in this way and the physician Luke preserved it for us today, is this not a truth to catch our attention? So often the modern church puts emphasis on actions speaking more loudly than words. And this can be true. As followers of Jesus Christ we should help feed and clothe the poor, and we should help build houses for those who don't have homes. The list of physical activities goes on and on, and I am in complete agreement that all of these acts of compassion can honor the Lord Jesus Christ. This passage should not only prompt us to use our Spirit-led natural abilities and talents, but it should also challenge us to use our Spirit-empowered gifts to advance Christ's kingdom. He gave them to us to enable us to reach a lost and hurting world.

One of the hindrances to a Spirit-led response to life can be caused by spiritual bondage in our lives. Over the past forty-seven years of walking in the ways of the Holy Spirit, I have been privileged to minister to thousands of people. I have found that there are many people whose lives are making an authentic impact in the kingdom of God, but who still struggle with evil spirits. Some have received this spiritual bondage through family lines; others have received it because their sins have opened them up to invasion. Some have received it because of the sins of others against them. Still others have been invaded just because of life's difficult circumstances. If any of this rings a bell in your spirit, you can come against this bondage in the authority and power of Jesus. This is called self-deliverance.

In Luke 8:1-2 we see Jesus going from one town and village to another proclaiming the good news of the kingdom of God. The twelve disciples were with him as were some women who had been cured of evil spirits and diseases. Mary Magdalene was among those women. Jesus had cast seven demons out of her. Did this ministry make a significant difference in Mary? In answering that question, consider this question: To whom did Jesus first appear after the resurrection? As we see in the Gospel of John (20:14), it was Mary Magdalene. She was one of the women in the faithful band of ladies who supported Jesus and His disciples financially and who traveled with them.

When the disciples fled upon Jesus' arrest, these faithful women stood firmly with Him. We know they were present at the crucifixion. This passage teaches us that some of these women had been delivered from evil spirits, and some had been healed from diseases. Of course, Jesus was the instrument of deliverance for those who had received deliverance, and healing for those who had received the miracle of healing.

Another truth is evident in this passage of Scripture. It says of Mary Magdalene that seven demons had come out of her. This statement teaches us that a person can have a number of demons and still function. How deeply Mary must have appreciated the freedom Jesus brought to her! She followed Him with courage and had the privilege of being the first person to see the risen Lord!

As did Matthew and Mark, Luke also speaks of the demon-possessed man from the region of the Gerasenes (Luke 8:26-39). One truth I would like to emphasize, as we again look at this event in the life of Jesus, is how the demon drove the man into solitary places. Often, I see a spirit in a believer that tries to isolate that believer from people who could really be of great help to the person. While I know that we are different personality types and some people love their solitude, I also know that spirits want to push us away from others.

We see the personality of the demons emerging as they begged Jesus repeatedly not to send them into the abyss. We can see the fear in the demons reflected in the fear of the man who was driven away from society and who had become a danger to himself because of the spirits. After the demons are cast out, the delivered man begged to follow along after Jesus. But with compassion for others in the area, Jesus tells him to return home and tell those people how much God has done for him. The Scripture reports that the man went away and told all over the town what had happened to him. We can imagine the amazement in the hearts of the people who had known him in his previous condition and now saw him in his right mind!

As someone who loves beautiful churches that are comfortable and well-maintained, I am moved by our Lord going against those traditions as He entered the land of the Gentiles, walked in an area in close proximity to hogs, and ministered to a man who lived in a graveyard. How He went against the conventional religious convictions of His day! As our example, He is in the position to call us to stand against the scripturally ungrounded conventional wisdom of our day.

As Mark also reported in his Gospel, we see in Luke 9:1-2 Jesus calling the twelve together and giving them power and authority to drive out all demons. He also sent them out to preach the kingdom of God and heal the sick. In this passage we again encounter Jesus' three primary ministries: healing the sick, casting out demons, and preaching the kingdom of God. So they went from village to village fulfilling His command.

Later, in Luke 9:26, Jesus says, *"Whoever is ashamed of Me and My words, the Son of Man will be ashamed of him when He comes in His glory, and the glory of the Father and of the holy angels."* Some of Jesus' actions do not appeal to a number of the intellectually sophisticated. But, He fulfilled the mission of His Father in heaven, who is the Ruler over all. May we never be ashamed of Jesus, His actions, or His words!

Jesus travels to a mountain with Peter, James, and John (Luke 9). Here they have a powerful encounter with Moses and Elijah who appear in glorious splendor and begin to converse with Jesus. As Peter voices a suggestion to them, a cloud appears and envelopes them all. A voice from the cloud declares, *"This is my Son, whom I have chosen; listen to him"* (Luke 9:35 NIV).

As the disciples and Jesus come down off the mountain the next day, they encounter a man from the gathered crowd who calls out, *"Teacher, I beg you to look at my son, for he is my only child. A spirit seizes him, and he suddenly screams; it throws him into convulsions so that he foams at the mouth…"* (Luke 9:38-39 NIV). Jesus rebukes the evil spirit, heals the boy, and gives him back to his father. The people were all amazed at the greatness of God!

We can only imagine the pain this father was experiencing as he saw his only child in such torment. When Jesus set the son free, the entire family experienced a new freedom. Often, it is not only an individual who suffers, but the whole family is affected because of the torment of one of its members as is seen in this passage. Hope is restored to a family when a very disruptive member receives deliverance.

When Jesus rebuked the evil spirit and healed the boy, Luke 9:43 (NIV) states that *"they were all amazed at the greatness of God…everyone was marveling at all that Jesus did…."* That is a goal for us! In my years of ministry I have only sometimes reached that goal. Many times people were helped, but often not in such a sudden, holy, spectacular way. We know from the book of Acts that the apostle's shadow would fall on people, and they would be healed or delivered. Also, personal garments from the apostles were taken to people, and they would be delivered.

We must realize that the same Holy Spirit who indwelled them indwells us! Jesus promised, *"Truly, truly, I say to you, he who believes in me, the works that I do, he will do also; and greater works than these he will do; because I go to the Father"* (John 14:12). My desire is to see broken lives transformed and for people to stand amazed at the greatness of our God. That is a goal worthy of all our service to the Lord.

Also in Luke 9 we see a very brief account of Jesus showing the importance of the ministry of deliverance. *"'Master,' said John, 'we saw someone driving out demons in your name and tried to stop him, because he is not one of us.' 'Do not stop him,' Jesus said, 'for whoever is not against you is for you'"* (Luke 9:49-50 NIV). John the apostle was defending their turf by trying to stop someone who was casting out demons but who was not one of the twelve disciples of Jesus. Jesus, appreciating what this ministry can do for people, said, "Don't stop them." Jesus wanted the ministry to flourish; He wanted it to reach far beyond the original twelve disciples.

One of my favorite accounts of the deliverance ministry is found in Luke 10. The Scripture says, *"After this, the Lord appointed seventy-two others* [some translations say seventy] *and sent them two by two ahead of him to every town and place where he was about to go"* (Luke 10:1 NIV). After ministering for a period of time the seventy-two returned with joy and said:

> *"Lord, even the demons submit to us in your name." He replied, "I saw Satan fall like lightning from heaven. I have given you authority to trample on snakes and scorpions and to overcome all the power of the enemy; nothing will harm you. However, do not rejoice that the spirits submit to you, but rejoice that your names are written in heaven"* (Luke 10:17-20 NIV).

The seventy-two were surprised, apparently greatly surprised, that the demons submitted to their commands in the authority of Jesus, and they rejoiced in that reality.

Jesus saw the future fall of Satan begin as His followers, unnamed disciples, were taking authority over the forces of darkness. Here is a group of faithful followers who had overcome the power of the enemy. Because of their reports, Jesus was full of joy through the Holy Spirit and said, *"I praise you, Father, Lord of heaven and earth...."* While He rejoiced, He exhorted them to rejoice in the profound truth that their names are written in heaven, instead of rejoicing in their ministry successes.

In Luke 13:10-17 (NIV), Luke, a physician, recounts a healing Jesus performed. He describes *"a woman...who had been crippled by a spirit for eighteen years. She was bent over and could not straighten up at all."* Challenged by narrow-minded religious leaders, Jesus demanded, *"…should not this woman, a daughter of Abraham, whom Satan has kept bound for eighteen long years, be set free on the Sabbath day from what bound her?"* What do we learn from this passage? Certainly we see Jesus' compassion, a compassion that led to a pitiful woman being healed. Jesus stated that she was a daughter of Abraham. Abraham was the father of the faithful. Jesus did not say, "Go and sin no more." She seemed to be a righteous woman, which is an indicator that a spirit can dwell in a righteous person. Also, we see that a spirit can cause some of our illnesses because the woman was clearly infirmed. The spirit came from Satan, so we know it did not like the woman. As we can see, this is an important passage to give us more understanding concerning forces of evil.

The Pharisees then reported to Jesus that Herod wanted to kill Him. They urged Him to leave Jerusalem, but Jesus answered them, *"…I will keep on driving out demons and healing people today and tomorrow, and on the third day I will reach my goal"* (Luke 13:32 NIV). Again, His mission is defined in part by deliverance. He spoke boldly to wicked Herod and declared His goal.

In Luke 22:3 we are told that Satan entered Judas and caused him to betray Jesus. It is my opinion that a human body could not contain Satan, a fallen angel. Therefore, one of Satan's demons entered Judas on his behalf. Judas became the world's most infamous traitor driven by a messenger of Satan. Destruction came upon someone who had had every opportunity to experience success because he had been with Jesus for three years. But all of that was lost when he was driven into the will of Satan.

THE LETTERS OF JOHN

The Gospel of John gives very little insight into the regime of darkness. John primarily focuses on the teachings of the Lord Jesus. It is therefore necessary to go to the letters of John to understand his inspired perspective on the demonic.

In First John 3:8 he writes, *"… The Son of God appeared for this purpose, to destroy the works of the devil."* One of the ways Jesus destroyed the works of the devil was to cast demons out of people, setting them free! These spirits hindered them from walking in righteousness.

First John 4:2-3 (NIV) states, *"…Every spirit that acknowledges that Jesus Christ has come in the flesh is from God, but every spirit that does not acknowledge Jesus is not from God."* John himself had cast out demons according to two of the gospel writers. He knew from long experience that spirits are real. Not only had he ministered in this impacting ministry, but he had seen his fellow apostles do the same. Still more importantly, he had observed his beloved Lord demonstrate His love to people by casting out spirits!

Often love does the hard thing; all of these founders of the Christian faith crushed the works of Satan under foot by driving spirits from people. We observe that at least twenty-one of the books that comprise the New Testament were written by leaders who cast out demons. Probably all the writers did, but we cannot be sure.

John writes in First John 5:19 (NIV) the following, *"We know that we are children of God, and that the whole world is under the control of the evil one."* Nothing has changed! Even though many have become authentic believers in Christ, the world is still under the control of the evil one. If you doubt me, watch the news tonight. Having said that, God is sovereign, and our God reigns!

THE BOOK OF ACTS

After the Lord ascended into heaven, His great work of deliverance continued through His followers. As the Holy Spirit was poured out upon them in the second chapter of Acts, they excitedly shared the good news of His resurrection and the new life that could be experienced because of the Lord's triumph. Also, the love Jesus had shown through the miracles He had performed was a major part of their ministry. Instead of being heroes, they again and again found themselves in serious trouble.

Peter and John were arrested because God enabled them to miraculously heal a crippled man. As Peter begins boldly proclaiming Christ to the gathered crowd, he and John are arrested but then later released. Upon returning to the gathered group of believers, they all begin praying, *"Stretch out your hand to heal and perform miraculous signs through the name of your holy servant Jesus"* (Acts 4:30 NIV). Were not some of these signs and wonders they earnestly were requesting the casting out of spirits? I think so! The Scripture continues, *"After they prayed, the place where they were meeting was shaken…"* (Acts 4:31 NIV). Surely God heard their prayer.

In Acts 5, a man named Ananias and his wife sold a piece of property and pretended to give all the proceeds to the church. Not only did they lie to the church leaders and to the people, they lied to the Holy Spirit. Peter challenged Ananias with the question, *"How is it that Satan has so filled your heart that you have lied to the Holy Spirit…?"* (Acts 5:3 NIV). Here was a professed follower of Christ whose heart was *"filled"* by Satan. Was it a spirit from Satan, or was it a consuming thought? Whatever the answer may be, God's justice prevailed.

As we continue to look at Acts 5, we see God at work through the apostles once again:

> *…people brought the sick into the streets and laid them on beds and mats so that at least Peter's shadow might fall on some of them as he passed by. Crowds gathered also from the towns around Jerusalem to bring their sick and those tormented by impure* [evil] *spirits, and all of them were healed* (Acts 5:15-16 NIV).

There was such an anointing on Peter that people were going to great lengths to receive healing and deliverance from the Lord through him. Again, we see a description of demon activity: the people were *"tormented by impure* [evil] *spirits."* Following his Lord's example, Peter was showing love and compassion to the people by not leaving them in tormenting bondage. He drove out the demons with the authority given him by Christ.

Philip, who is called one of the first deacons in the early church, is sent by the Lord to minister in the area of Israel named Samaria. A powerful awakening occurs. In Acts 8:6-8 (NIV) we read the following: *"When the crowds heard Philip and saw the signs he performed, they all paid close attention to what he said. For with shrieks, impure spirits came out of many…. So there was great joy in that city."* The clearest picture of an awakening in the New Testament is what happened in Samaria.

Although, our focus is on spiritual warfare, it is good to note that all kinds of miracles happened in this place, including the greatest miracle of all. Many came to salvation in Christ! Could evil spirits have been one of the barriers to faith in Christ? I know so!

It is my opinion that the next great awakening will have as one of its focuses the casting out of demons. Also of note, Philip was not one of the original apostles. That fact did not stop the Holy Spirit from powerfully using him. If this could happen in the first century, it can and often does happen in this century!

Peter is called to preach at the home of Cornelius. As Peter proclaims Christ, He declares the following in Acts 10:37-38 (NIV), *"You know what has happened… how God anointed Jesus of Nazareth with the Holy Spirit and power, and how he went around doing good and healing all who were under the power of the devil, because God was with him."* Here is a description of Jesus' activities by one of the people who knew Him best. He acted out of the goodness of His heart; He freed those who were under the power of the devil.

I ask you a question: Are we, you and I, supposed to exhibit the goodness of Jesus? Then, what about rescuing those under the power of darkness? Oh, if only the godly would awaken to this truth and embrace the power of the Holy Spirit so freely given; how the church and even society would change!

While there are many personalities introduced to us in the book of Acts, the two dominant figures are Peter and Paul. Peter is the outstanding figure in the first half of the book, and Paul is the dominant figure in the second half of this historical account of the early church. In the preceding paragraphs, we have looked at Peter's ministry to those bound by spirits. Now let's look at Paul's authority over spirits of darkness.

In Acts 16:16-18 (NIV) we see Paul at work:

> *Once when we were going to the place of prayer, we were met by a female slave who had a spirit by which she predicted the future. She earned a great deal of money for her owners by fortune-telling. She followed Paul and the rest of us, shouting, "These men are servants of the Most High God, who are telling you the way to be saved." She kept this up for many days. Finally Paul became so annoyed that he turned around and said to the spirit, "In the name of Jesus Christ I command you to come out of her!" At that moment the spirit left her.*

The slave girl sounded so religious. She was calling so much attention to Paul and his companions that she was disrupting what the Holy Spirit was doing through them. She was like a "barker" at a state fair calling attention to a sideshow. Did Paul hope she would be changed by the good news he was proclaiming? Maybe, but finally his patience came to an end. He cast out the demon that drove the girl.

A fortune-telling spirit falls under the category of the occult. From my experience of ministering in deliverance, anyone who has involved himself or herself in the occult needs deliverance. Satan loves his hoards to enter people as they naively pursue the supernatural, which, in turn, leads these people deeper into his control.

People in Christian leadership should try to be sure that those who promote their churches, ministries, and organizations should be doing so with the right Spirit motivating them. This passage shows the extreme of the wrong spirit promoting ministry.

Paul travels to Ephesus in Acts 19. In verses 11 and 12 we see these words, *"God did extraordinary miracles through Paul, so that even handkerchiefs and aprons that had touched him were taken to the sick, and their illnesses were cured and the evil spirits left them"* (NIV). The Scripture calls these miracles extraordinary because of the anointing from the accomplished work of the Lord Jesus that rested upon Paul.

Like you and me, Paul was an imperfect human; he was flesh and blood. But, oh how the Lord used him to free others! Just think, if Christ used you to cast a spirit from someone, then you have been used by the Lord to cause a miracle to happen! For Paul, to cast out a spirit was a miracle; for his clothes to touch someone and deliverances happen was an extraordinary miracle. The absolute wonder of it all! We may never be so used that the word *extraordinary* would describe our ministry, but we can still trod the works of Satan underfoot by casting out spirits.

In the very next verse Luke tells us that some Jews were going around attempting to cast out demons. Success was not their strong suit. This was not a negative statement about Jews because Paul was a Jew. Their lack of success was because they were not personally connected to Jesus Christ. Attempting to use a secondhand faith, they declared, *"In the name of the Jesus whom Paul preaches, I command you to come out."* Secondhand faith did not work. The demon speaking through the man answered, *"Jesus I know, and Paul I know about, but who are you?"* (See Acts 19:13,15 NIV.) Demons have knowledge; that fact is evident from this passage. Also, they have will and personality; they drove the man to attack the Jews. Scripture call us to be participants in this ministry, but we must have a personal relationship with Christ before undertaking such a step. Authority over demons comes from Him!

THE EPISTLES

1 and 2 Corinthians

The apostles continue to advance Christ's kingdom. As the Spirit raised up groups of Christians, the apostles began to write letters to these believers. These epistles gave them and us more instruction about forces of darkness. Church leadership did not want the believers, many of them new believers, to be ignorant of their enemy.

Paul, troubled about abuses surrounding Holy Communion in the church at Corinth, spoke of his concern in his first letter to them. In First Corinthians 10:20-21 (NIV) he says, *"…the sacrifices of pagans are offered to demons, not to God, and I do not want you to be participants with demons. You cannot drink the cup of the Lord and the cup of demons, too; you cannot have a part of both the Lord's table and the table of demons."*

Some Christians want to pass this statement off as the culture of antiquity or as figurative language. I believe Paul was speaking literally. Extreme abuse of Communion was as if the participants were involved with demons. Remember, the apostle was writing to a beloved Christian church. Great abuses can open the way for dark forces inside and outside the church. The most intellectual leader in the New Testament addressed this problem for all to see.

A person can sometimes worship demons as that person participates in religions that are not based upon the accomplished work of the Lord Jesus Christ. Let me emphasize again that involvement with the occult, New Age, or superstitions can, in actuality, be worshiping demons. After having ministered to many university graduates, I can say that it is not only the developing nations that need the ministry of deliverance—there is a great need in the Western world as well.

Paul begins the twelfth chapter of First Corinthians (NIV) with these words, *"Now about the gifts of the Spirit, brothers and sisters, I do not want you to be uninformed."* He continues in verse 7, *"Now to each one the manifestation of the Spirit is given for the common good."* Finally, in verse 10, this phrase appears in a list of the gifts of the Spirit, *"...to another distinguishing between spirits...."* The apostle wanted the Corinthian Church to know about the gifts the Holy Spirit given to the body of Christ. In this list he records nine of those gifts. This seventh gift is of special importance to our study.

In this list are some of the gifts we value deeply in the body of Christ, such as knowledge, wisdom, and faith. If the gifts of knowledge, wisdom, and faith are still greatly valued by Christians, we should also value discernments of spirits. It is one of the gifts given *"for the common good."* This means that it is a help to the body of Christ. It can be an evangelistic tool. But far more importantly, it can be a mighty help in freeing individual believers from bondages and allowing them to have the freedom they long to experience. Let's explore this gift of discernments of spirits further.

I have become aware of two basic uses of this gift. The first is the discerning of the attitude and the emotion of a group of people. Are they hungry to learn, are they pensive, or are they preoccupied with other matters? This insight from the Holy Spirit can be helpful in communicating with a group. The second way this gift operates is by enabling a person to have God-given insight into bondage from darkness. With this insight a person who ministers can discern and drive out forces of darkness.

It is amazing to observe the incredible accuracy of a person using this gift. The person ministering can call out spirits from an individual whom he or she has never met with the accuracy of a person who has known the individual for twenty years. Paul, under the inspiration of the Holy Spirit, listed this gift among the other eight because, like us, they needed it! It was a gift for the life of the church as were the other listed gifts.

Paul wrote a second letter to the Corinthians in which he instructs them and us in spiritual warfare. In Second Corinthians 10:4 (NIV) he wrote, *"The weapons we fight with are not the weapons of the world. On the contrary, they have divine power to demolish strongholds."* Notice that Paul says, *"we fight with."* He and his band of brothers were not limited only to their persuasive arguments. They caused ministry to happen. Nor were these weapons limited in their use by only a few. They were given to the body of Christ. They enabled those early Christians, and us, to move in the realm of the Spirit to bring down strongholds of darkness.

In Second Corinthians 11:4 (NIV) Paul confronts, *"If someone comes to you and preaches a Jesus other than the Jesus we preached, or if you receive a different spirit from the Spirit you received, or a different gospel from the one you accepted, you put up with it easily enough."* The apostle is challenging them about welcoming a substitute Jesus, a substitute gospel, or a different spirit from the Holy Spirit. To believers he spoke of receiving a false spirit. If this could be reality in the first century, could it be any less reality in the twenty-first century? You continue to see why we who do this ministry take it so seriously.

Galatians

In the epistle to the Galatians, Paul asks the following question in 3:1, *"Who has bewitched you?"* Because of the way this question is asked, it appears to be more than human error. Paul seems to be asking the church what spirit had deceived them. He could not believe the report that had come to him about the Galatian Christians. They had strayed from basic Christianity.

He says of the church in Galatians 4:8 (NIV) the following, *"...you were slaves to those who by nature are not gods."* He could be speaking to their worship of idols, or he could be speaking of their worship of spirits. Probably he was referencing both idols and spirits. The ancient world was very conscience of the spirit world. The modern world, because of pseudo-sophistication and fear, chooses not to pay much attention to the world of spiritual beings. It is our loss that this is true. If a person approaches the spirit world in the security of God the Creator, he or she is the better for it. An illustration of this is found in the New Testament where the people approach darkness with realism and faith and were victorious for themselves and brought great freedom to many others!

In addressing the church at Ephesus, Paul writes in Ephesians 6:11-12 (NIV):

> *Put on the full armor of God, so that you can take your stand against the devil's schemes. For our struggle is not against flesh and blood, but against the rulers, against the authorities, against the powers of this dark world and against the spiritual forces of evil in the heavenly realms.*

Here is a clear picture of the hierarchy, the spiritual hosts that oppose God's people. The devil is referenced in verse 11. He is the head of the great hosts of darkness. Then rulers, authorities, powers, spiritual forces of evil are listed. Apparently the devil is the head of forces that rule over forces that rule over forces. The amazing truth is that we can stand against the devil's schemes! In Christ, we do not have to fear this host! A 300-pound, all-pro defensive lineman can be greatly frightened by a 3-pound rattlesnake. Yet, if that professional football player has on snake-proof boots and carries a garden hoe, he has nothing to fear.

Colossians

In Colossians 2:10 (NIV) we read these words, *"In Christ you have been brought to fullness. He is the head over every power and authority."* In Colossians 2:15 (NIV) Paul states, *"Having disarmed the powers and authorities, he made a public spectacle of them, triumphing over them by the cross."* What finally defeats the powers of darkness? It is the cross of Christ. Through His death and resurrection, He has given us the authority necessary to defeat forces of darkness.

We do not have to pretend they don't exist; we do not have to fear them. We have victory over them because of Jesus' victory over death! I urge you to continue to learn to apply what Christ has accomplished on the cross; do as He did. Tread the works of Satan underfoot.

Paul is writing to Christians, challenging them to walk in favor with the Lord and seeking that they support his ministry in prayer. In Second Thessalonians 3:2-5, he requests prayer that the message of the Lord might spread rapidly and that he might be honored in his ministry. He also asks the believers to pray that he be protected from wicked and evil men. He commends the believers in Thessalonica for doing well and adjures them to continue in obedience. In the midst of this paragraph he states, *"The Lord is faithful, and He will strengthen and protect you from the evil one."* Just as Paul needed to exert himself in the various aspects of his ministry, so these Greek Christians needed to exert themselves against the evil one and his forces.

1 and 2 Timothy

In his first letter to his beloved Timothy, Paul states: *"Here is a trustworthy saying: Whoever aspires to be an overseer desires a noble task. …He must also have a good reputation with outsiders, so that he will not fall into disgrace and into the devil's trap"* (1 Timothy 3:1,7 NIV). As church leaders were selected, Timothy was instructed to choose people *"who would not fall into disgrace and the devil's trap."* Church leaders, like church members, have traps set for them to cause disgrace to Christ's kingdom. Any of us who have walked with the Lord very long know this to be a reality.

In First Timothy 4:1 (NIV), Paul writes again to his spiritual son, *"The Spirit clearly says that in later times some will abandon the faith and follow deceiving spirits and things taught by demons."* Surely we live in the later times. A person could write a book on what deceiving spirits do. Another book could be written on things taught by demons. Endless are the minefields that people have walked into because of deceiving spirits. Non-measurable is the destruction that has been caused by people influenced by demons teaching falsehood. It is wise to guard your heart and your mind. I encourage you to take spiritual forces as seriously as did Paul.

James and Peter

We move to the book of James. James references darkness in several verses. In 2:19 (NIV) he writes, *"You believe that there is one God. Good! Even the demons believe that—and shudder."* In 4:7 (NIV) we read these words, *"Submit yourselves, then, to God. Resist the devil, and he will flee from you."* James acknowledges that the demonic is real. He even used them to make the spiritual point that demons believe God is real. James is stating here that one must not only believe in God but must also obey God and submit to His lordship over his life to have a relationship with Him! In that context, we can have victory over the devil and his forces by resisting him.

As we continue our search for references to the demonic in the epistles, we now look at First Peter 5:8-9 (NIV). Peter states, *"Your enemy the devil prowls around like a roaring lion looking for someone to devour. Resist him, standing firm in the faith...."* Since the devil cannot be everywhere at once—only God is omnipresent—he uses multitudes of demons to accomplish his attempt to devour the righteous. Peter's answer is to resist him, or his representative, that tries to devour you.

Peter continues by saying to his readers and to us also, to stand firm in the faith. Therefore, you and I are exhorted to resist demonic forces and to stand firm with the faith God has given us when darkness assails us. It was reality then; it is reality now. It was good, inspired advice then; it is good, inspired advice now!

Jude

As we look into the book of Jude, we see an awesome encounter between the archangel Michael and the devil. Jude is referencing an event that happened approximately 1,400 years before Christ. The great leader Moses has died, and a debate ensues over what should happen to his body. In this dispute, Michael does not bring a slanderous accusation against the devil. The victory was won in this encounter as he said, *"The Lord rebuke you!"* What is clear from this encounter is that Michael's authority came from the Lord who gave him the victory over the devil. The same truth applies to us today; our victory over the forces of darkness that would attempt to rule over us is accomplished as we stand in the strength of the Lord.

REVELATION

Many excellent books have been written on the last book in the Bible. I will point out only a few references from Revelation, the book that speaks most about forces of darkness. We see the following in Revelation 9:20 (NIV), *"...They did not stop worshiping demons and idols of gold, silver, bronze, stone, and wood...."* In Revelation 12:7 (NIV) we see, *"Then war broke out in heaven. Michael and his angels fought against the dragon, and the dragon and his angels fought back."* Revelation 18:2 states, *"...Fallen! Fallen is Babylon the Great! She has become a dwelling for demons and a haunt for every impure* [evil] *spirit...."*

In Revelation we see in vivid language the cosmic battle between the forces on God's side versus the forces on the side of Satan. You know who wins!

As we finish our brief journey through Scripture, the question may be asked, "If this ministry was so essential to the New Testament church, why was not more said about it in the epistles?" I have a several-part answer to that good question.

First, as you have seen, there were a number of references to dark spiritual beings in the epistles. But the epistles mainly focus on governance, correct doctrine, relationships, etc. Much of the day-to-day ministry is not discussed at length. The ministry of deliverance had been mastered by those who paved the way for the gospel to be spread to many lands. It was not necessary for Paul and the other writers of the epistles to emphasize this ministry. Unlike our way of sharing faith, deliverance happened as the gospel was preached, not years later when the believer struggled to walk in faith.

For Paul and the other writers of the epistles, it was enough that they reminded the believers that they faced opposition from several fronts: from secular quarters, from false religions, and from spiritual forces. They exhorted the believers to stand firm, to be on the alert, to take up weapons of spiritual warfare. I am sure they remembered verbal accounts of Jesus and the original twelve casting out spirits.

The person of Satan was introduced to us in the third chapter of Genesis. We have then seen evil spirits introduced in the Saul-David conflict a thousand years before Christ, which is approximately 3,000 years before our present time. We have looked at examples of Jesus casting out demons and confronting Satan. We have seen the early church follow in His footsteps to confront the demonic. Opposition to the righteous literally appears from the first book of the Bible until the last book of the Bible.

Starting in the Old Testament and continuing through to the very last book in the New Testament, we have seen Scripture writers expose the work of Satan and his host. While this is only one of the many themes that these writers teach us, it is important that we understand the reality of forces of darkness around us. They can harass and invade our loved ones and our friends. Yes, they can invade us! But there is an answer, and it is found in the work and person of our Lord Jesus Christ!

QUESTIONS TO CONSIDER

1. In the Deuteronomy 18 passage, the Israelites were warned not to imitate the destructive and occult practices of the pagans that the Lord was driving out of the land. In what ways might we be tempted to imitate evil for the purpose of entertainment?

2. Have you ever considered that séances, horoscopes, and Ouija boards fall under God's definition of detestable?

3. What were Jesus' three primary ministries?

4. What does Jesus say defines that the kingdom of God has actually come (Matthew 12:28)?

5. Were you surprised to discover so many references in the New Testament to deliverance and/or demons?

PRAYER

Father, forgive me when I have unwittingly participated in activities that You call detestable and are abominations to You! Forgive me for any involvement in the occult, whether it be reading my horoscope, having my fortune told, or playing with a Ouija board. Continue to teach me and give me wisdom.

I praise You. I thank You for being a good, good Father who gives good gifts to His children. Thank You for the gifts of the Holy Spirit that enable us to minister in Your name. Thank You for the weapons of spiritual warfare with which we can battle against the forces of evil and darkness. Thank You for giving us power and authority to drive out demons in Your name. Increase our faith. In Jesus' name, amen.

Chapter Eleven

FROM MY BOOKSHELVES: INSIGHTS FROM TRUSTED SOURCES

For by wise guidance you will wage war, and in abundance of counselors there is victory (Proverbs 24:6).

The following is a sampling of writings from other authors on the important subject before us. A few of these authors might take exception with some of my conclusions, but most are in agreement with the positions I state in this book. As you will see, all believe in the existence of demons. No one takes the position that they have no influence in our lives; they haven't just disappeared to reappear at the very end of the last times. They are active in our world today.

In this smorgasbord of writers, you will see that the subject is written about by a number of people, but the topic seems to be left out of mainstream Christianity. It is my hope that we may awaken the church to the value of this ministry in the present and in the future.

In preparing resources for this book, I am surprised with the support coming from scholars in their writings that authenticate the existence of demons. Scholar after scholar believes in their existence. They support the fact that Jesus dealt with real personalities. They also believe that all of this did not end in the first century, but that truths revealed in the New Testament have value for today.

I continue to be puzzled how the belief system of scholars often does not reach the classroom and the pulpit. I know this theme has surfaced several times in my writing, but I marvel that a major biblical theme is underrepresented in preaching and teaching today. I optimistically expect there to be major changes in this area in the future.

DEREK PRINCE

The following story came from the writings of Derek Prince, a former Cambridge professor whom I was privileged to know. He was a man of integrity and great scholarship. This account is abbreviated from the original writing.

> I met a Jewish lady named Miriam who was a believer in Jesus. She personally told me her testimony. She was a capable executive secretary and was given a high paying job working for the president of a particular business. She soon discovered that he and all the executives of the company were in a strange cult led by a guru.

> "The guru has pronounced blessings over us, and we would like you to type them out for us," her boss directed. When Miriam started to type, she discovered that they were in fact fortune-telling, with occult overtones. As a committed Christian, she didn't feel free to type this material so she went to her boss and explained the situation. [Derek guesses that the guru heard about this incident and spoke some kind of curse against Miriam. This would be a channel for occult power.]

> Almost immediately Miriam began to develop acute arthritis in both hands. Her fingers curled up and became absolutely stiff and rigid. She could not

bend them. She could not work. The pain was agonizing. A physician diagnosed the condition as rheumatoid arthritis.

A Christian friend of this executive secretary heard my three messages, Curses, Causes, and Cure and brought the cassettes to Miriam. On the third cassette where I lead people in a prayer of release from the curse over their lives, the cassette jammed. It would not go forward, it would not go back, it would not eject.

The friend who had brought the cassette had a printed version of the prayer of release. Miriam read the prayer out loud. Her fingers uncurled and became completely flexible. The pain ceased. By the time Miriam had finished praying the prayer, she was perfectly healed. She went back to the same doctor and had him check her hands again. His diagnosis was that medically she was totally healed.

This came by only one thing. There was no prayer for healing. There was just a prayer of release from a curse. [Taken from *Blessings and Curses: Biblical Truth Simply Explained* by Derek Prince, published by Chosen Books, 2003.]

Derek Prince also wrote on the subject "How to Keep Your Deliverance" in one of his books. The following are some excerpts from that chapter:

Here are some basic principles to help you rebuild your life. The first is live by God's word. In Matthew 4 Jesus said that all mankind shall live "by every word that proceeds from the mouth of God." The word *live* is all inclusive, covering everything we think, say or do. It is best summed up in three phrases: think the Word of God; speak the word of God; and act upon the word of God.

Secondly, put on the garment of praise. In Isaiah 61 God offers us the "garment of praise" to replace "the spirit of heaviness." [Derek relates how he was delivered from depression when it was identified as a spirit of heaviness. After that he gradually learned that when he was praising the Lord, the spirit of heaviness would not come near him. He writes that he needed to cultivate a lifestyle in which praise would cover him as completely as the clothes he wore.]

Thirdly, be disciplined. Jesus' last order to His apostles was to go…and make disciples…as seen in Matthew 28. A disciple, as the word indicates, is one who is under discipline…. It is true that deliverance brings us freedom, but many Christians misunderstand the nature of freedom. We have been freed, but we are not free to do our own thing; we are freed that we may bring our lives under God's discipline.

Fourthly, cultivate right fellowship. We need to recognize that one of the most powerful influences in our lives is the people with whom we associate. This means we have to choose the kind of people we spend time with. There is no place for self-centered individualism in the Christian life. As Christians we need each other. If you sincerely desire to keep your deliverance, you must break off relationships that have a wrong influence on you, and begin to cultivate friends who will encourage you and set for you a good example. [Taken from *They Shall Expel Demons: What You Need to Know about Demons, Your Invisible Enemies* by Derek Prince, published by Chosen Books, 1998; pages 220–223.]

Referencing Acts 16:16-18 Derek Prince writes of the discerning of spirits. He speaks of the encounter with Paul the apostle and the girl who had a fortune-telling spirit.

Every word the girl said was true; she was advertising the preachers of the gospel, but an evil spirit was doing it through her. Paul discerned this and cast the spirit out of her. We must have the same kind of discernment today. Fortune-telling demons are in the church. As I go to even nice "respectable" church congregations, I encounter the demon of divination among people who are fooling around with horoscopes, Ouija boards, and astrology. They become "hooked" by the same demon of divination, as did the girl in Acts 16.

The gift of discerning of spirits is very important to the functioning of the body of Christ. It results in believers recognizing the presence of the Holy Spirit and the ways in which God is working, it reveals the character and motivations of the human heart, and it identifies the evil spirits which are the cause of sickness and strife. When discerning of spirits is operating on a full scale in the body of Christ, it will bring remarkable ministry to the church in the world. [Taken from *The Gifts of the Spirit* by Derek Prince, published by Whitaker House, 2007; page 103.]

DON BASHAM

In a classic book on the subject of spiritual warfare, Don Bashan told an engaging story from his own ministry. I will retell it in an abbreviated form.

One evening Alice and I were having dinner with a group of friends in West Palm Beach. Over coffee the conversation came around to the subject of deliverance. The hostess suddenly banged her fist on the table, rattling the dishes and startling all of us. "That's the biggest bunch of nonsense I have heard," she exclaimed. "I don't believe a word of it, besides, it's a perfectly loathsome subject to bring up at a dinner table."

The lady was trembling and her eyes began to fill with tears. She jumped up from the table and rushed from the room. Her husband, his face red with embarrassment, murmured an apology about his wife having trouble with her nerves lately.

"Basham, you've done it again!" I silently berated myself. Aloud I said, "I had no idea this conversation would upset anyone. Please forgive me for causing such a scene." The husband tried to reassure me. "It's not your fault. My wife has been nervous lately."

The lady rejoined the company. "I want to apologize to everyone," she said. "I wonder, Don, if you would pray for me?" I began with the words, "In the name of Jesus, I come against any evil spirit in this…" With a startled cry she jumped to her feet and almost shouted the words, "No, no I don't want you casting anything out of me! I just wanted you to say a prayer."

It seemed to me that the evening was ruined. I had spoiled a dinner party. When we left a few minutes later, I felt like an outcast.

The next morning, I received a phone call from one of the women who had been there. "I thought you'd like to know what happened last night! After you and your wife left, the lady changed her mind about needing deliverance. They asked me to pray with them. Frankly, I was scared stiff, but I agreed anyhow. I commanded an evil spirit to come out of her. She gave a kind of a little cough and started crying—crying for joy. You wouldn't believe the change in her! She looked absolutely radiant. Do you think it really was a deliverance?"

I did think so! I could see tremendous possibility for the future right at that moment. I could see the possibility of the Church enabled to claim Jesus' promise that when the Son sets us free we are free indeed! [Taken from *Deliver Us from Evil* by Don Basham, published by Chosen Books, 2014; pages 123–124.]

Some of Pastor Basham's insights on how to know if one needs deliverance are as follows:

Test your hang-up first as a simple carnal sin and see what happens. Confess it, ask forgiveness, and believe that forgiveness has been granted. Now apply will, discipline, and prayer to the habit patterns that have entrenched themselves in this area. Whenever they reappear, put them "under the crucifixion" of Jesus, knowing that He is able when we are not. If all of this produces no victory, you may be dealing with a demon—and you should seek deliverance.

The modern term *hang-up* may be descriptive of demonic activity. Are we stuck at a point in our spiritual development? Is the problem subject to prayer and obedience? If not, we should at least consider demons as a cause.

If we ever feel compelled to destructive acts, it may be that an evil spirit is at work.

An especially strong negative reaction to the idea of deliverance should raise the question, "Where does this reaction come from?" Certainly there are realistic objections to this ministry; are these objections based on realism, or are they coming from another source—perhaps the demon themselves? [Taken from *Deliver Us from Evil* by Don Basham, pages 122, 124–125.]

DR. DAVID APPLEBY

The following are quotes from a paper presented to the American Association of Christian Counselors entitled *Deliverance as Part of the Therapeutic Process:*

Deliverance—the process by which a demonic spirit's influence over an individual is broken and the freedom to choose is restored. Deliverance does not make a person holy: it just removes the spiritual personality that influences a person towards evil.

Most Christians seek to deal with their sinful passions and desires through different spiritual disciplines such as prayer, fasting, meditation, Scripture reading, etc. In most cases this reduces the power of the flesh so that the word of God can be more easily followed. However, some believers discover that even after they have done all they know to do, they cannot seem to bring some areas of their lives under the will of God. One possible explanation is the phenomenon of demonization. Calling something "flesh" which really is demonic will only result in endless frustration on the part of the individual, and an improper treatment strategy on the part of the counselor.

Have no illusions. No demon will ever leave because you tell it to go. You have within yourself absolutely no power or authority to bring about a supernatural work of any kind. With helplessness come humility and a sense of absolute dependence upon the Holy Spirit. Command the demon to leave, stating the basis for your authority over the demon again and again, namely the death and resurrection of Jesus, His shedding His blood for our forgiveness, His victory over sin and death, etc. Eventually the demon will have to yield.

Dr. Appleby gives us the following insights in his book *It's Only a Demon:*

Sometimes, when things are difficult, it is helpful if the client leads the attack on the demonic spirit. There is nothing quite as powerful as a demonized individual rebuking the demon and telling it that it has to go. Few people can do this at the start of the deliverance, but many, after having several demons leave, begin to recognize the power of the blood and the power of the name of Jesus. They have experienced the power of that name first-hand. When the client begins to move in his or her own authority, it is not uncommon to find that little assistance is needed. The client finds out the demon's name, renounces it, confesses, and repents of having invited it in and casts it out.

This is most effective after several demonic spirits have left and their stronghold is considerably weakened. It is an especially valuable experience because it prepares the client for resisting demonic spirits in the days following the deliverance. They have learned the power they have over demonic spirits because of their personal experience during deliverance. [Taken from *It's Only a Demon: A Model of Christian Deliverance* by Dr. David W. Appleby, MDiv, MA, PhD, PhD, published by Spiritual Interventions Press, 2017, page 257.]

I have been privileged to have Dave as a houseguest and to minister with him in deliverance several times. He is for real!

DR. CHARLES H. KRAFT

Dr. Charles Kraft wrote the book *Defeating Dark Angels*, and in it states:

Our Western compartmentalized approach to healing isn't working. People with physical problems consult physicians and often are not healed because the underlying malady is not treated. People go to psychologists for emotional difficulties and often are not healed because spiritual factors are overlooked. If we are to work efficiently with God for complete healing, we need to take a comprehensive approach to those who hurt, working with the whole person, not just one part of the person.

Our task is to discover the deeper problem and claim the power of the Holy Spirit to bring to it whatever healing God desires to bring.... A client may complain of a splitting headache, plus other physical problems, but soon reveal that she hates herself, is angry and bitter toward her parents and husband (emotional problems), feels deeply guilty over certain things in her life, and is unforgiving towards those who have hurt her (spiritual problems). She may, in addition, be living under the influence of demons of death, hate, rejection, guilt, control, and many more. [Taken from *Defeating Dark Angels: Breaking Demonic Oppression in the Believer's Life* by Charles H. Kraft, published by Chosen Books, 2016; pages 83–84.]

Dr. Kraft relates another story in *Defeating Dark Angels:*

> A friend of mine was chatting with a woman who recently had been converted to Christianity out of the occult. While serving Satan, she had been able to "see" the amount of spiritual power people carry with them. According to her, every person carries a certain amount of spiritual power, but the difference in power between Christians and non-Christians is amazing. Indeed, she could spot a Christian in any group, even at a great distance, by noting the amount of spiritual power he or she carried. She now knows that the reason for this difference is the presence of the Holy Spirit in a believer.
>
> She remarked, though, that she and her occult group felt no threat from most Christians, even though they knew Christians were more powerful than they were. For the Christians had no idea how to use the power within them. Though that power (that is, the Holy Spirit, who is the source of their power) afforded them much protection from evil power, they did not know how to use the Holy Spirit's power to go on the offensive in spiritual warfare. [*Defeating Dark Angels*, page 91.]

Dr. Charles Kraft, professor emeritus from Fuller Seminary, gives this illustration from the experience of someone who once was on the "other side." The account continues from the woman who was in the occult that there were some Christians who *did* know how to use their power. The occult group learned to stay clear of these Christians.

Good Bible dictionaries have been a real source of biblical information for me through the years. Again and again I've turned to them as a resource in subjects of importance to me. So, once again I have gone to my library to draw information from dictionaries that might be helpful to you.

NEW BIBLE DICTIONARY

The following is from the *New Bible Dictionary*, page 270:

In the New Testament, the word *demons* always refer to spiritual beings hostile to God and men. Beelzebub is their prince so they may be regarded as his agents. The Gospels picture Jesus as in continual conflict with evil spirits. To cast out such beings from men is not easy. His opponents recognized both that He did this and, also, that it required a power greater than human power to do so. This is behind the stinging accusation that Jesus had a demon. Those who opposed His ministry tried to link him with forces of evil, instead of recognizing his divine origin. Therefore, they attributed His success to the indwelling of Satan. (I would add this is the greatest of all blasphemies!) The victory that Jesus won over demons He shared with His followers. When he sent out the twelve, He gave them power and authority over all demons and to cure diseases.

NEW DICTIONARY OF THEOLOGY

The following is taken from the *New Dictionary of Theology*, pages 197 and 245:

The New Testament writers believed demons were Satan's minions; were potential objects of worship; could speak through those they inhabited; could also possess animals; could cause suffering; could grant superhuman strength; could deceive Christians; and needed to be withstood by Christians. Paul sometimes uses the phrase "principalities and powers" to describe evil spiritual beings which oppose God and, potentially, are able to separate the Christian from God. Paul also associates idols with demons.

Jesus saw his ministry, particularly of exorcism, as the first of a two-stage defeat of Satan. In Paul and John's theology, the cross was the focus of the defeat. Jesus believed that the final defeat would be at the end of the age.

John Calvin refuted those who babble of devils as nothing else than evil emotions by pointing to texts where the reality of Satan and the devils (i.e. demons) is assured. The devil was an angel whose malice came as result of his revolt and fall. Calvin believes the writings tell us to arouse ourselves to take precaution against their stratagems.

A brief look at the early church after the New Testament is seen in the following quotes:

> The charismatic understanding of the authority to exorcise demons using the name of Jesus continued for some time in the post-apostolic period. A letter from Cornelius of Rome in 252 shows that the exorcist had become one of the orders of the clergy. By the 6th century the exorcist received a book of formulae containing prayers and adulations." And so it continues until this day.

A lengthy stream of discussion follows giving the positions of modern churches on the issue. The article concludes with the following:

> Despite hesitations among theologians and church hierarchies the practice of exorcism has increased in recent years in almost all denominations in response to pastoral needs.

EERDMAN'S DICTIONARY OF THE BIBLE

New Testament writers see demons as:

> Beings who in their true nature are agents of Satan and whose mission is to oppose the work of God and His people.... Demons feature prominently as adversaries in the ministry of Jesus, and as agents of Satan that must be overcome if Jesus' ministry is to be successful. Jesus Himself speaks of having come to plunder Satan's goods. Expulsion of demons from people is one means by which Jesus does so in the gospel accounts. Early Judaism had also taught that when the Messiah comes, he will overthrow the kingdom of Satan.

According to early Christian literature, demons do not operate in a vacuum; they oppress, attacking people from without, or possess, entering in an individual's body and attacking it from within. They cause disease and sickness all kinds although all sickness may not be attributed to them. The presence of a demon in a person might sometimes not be obvious to a third-party unless confronted by an exorcist. [Taken from *Eerdmans Dictionary of the Bible*, pages 337–338.]

DR. WALTER A. ELWELL

While I was preparing to use the following source, a very influential pastor in our city came to spend some time with me. He saw the book that I will now quote from and commented, "The editor was my professor in college." I answered, "I knew him because he married a girl from the college I attended." It's good to have personal contacts with scholars. Maybe some of their scholarship will rub off on us.

When demons were created, how they came to be demonic, and their organizational structure are not given significant attention in Scripture because the focus throughout the Bible is on God and His work in Christ rather than on the demonic attempts to demean that work....

The biblical word generally translated as demon-possession does not convey the English concept of possession (either ownership or eternal destiny) as much as it does the temporary control (under the power of the demons)....

The term most commonly used for the expulsion of demons in the New Testament is "cast out." In classic and Old Testament usage it had the sense of forcibly driving out an enemy. In the New Testament it is typically used of a physical removal; demons were cast out by the spirit of God....

Concerning exorcism we see the following:

> An exorcism implies a particular ritual, and Jesus, as well as the early church, relied on authority rather than ritual. It is not surprising, then, that nowhere in the New Testament is a Christian ritual for exorcism seen.

In the epistles:

> There is a shift from direct power encounters with demons to a focus of knowing and correctly applying the truth to thwart demonic influence.... Demons remain under God's sovereignty and can be used by Him to affect the divine plan. As Christians we are to submit ourselves to God to resist attacks of Satan and his host.

> While experience is not the final arbiter of doctrinal formation, our experience should be in accordance with our doctrine. Thus, it is reasonable to conclude that Christians may demonized and that the warnings to stand against Satan are not just to stop his attacks against the church or his control over those who do not believe. [Taken from the *Baker Theological Dictionary of the Bible* edited by Walter A. Elwell, published by Baker Academic, 2001; pages 163–165.]

THE NEW INTERNATIONAL DICTIONARY OF NEW TESTAMENT THEOLOGY

> The New Testament word that is translated *drive out*, can also be translated *expelled*, *send out*, or *take out*. It is used 81 times in the New Testament.

> The word has a theological bearing only in connection with casting out demons. Jesus and the early church shared the conceptions of their contemporaries about demons. But while the pagans and Jews of their contemporary

world environment tried to drive out demons by magic, exorcisms and other magical practices, Jesus needed only His word of command.

The driving out of demons was as much an accomplishment of His proclamation as were His acts of healing. Because Jesus with the authority of God showed Himself stronger, the demon had to yield to Him and bow to His power. In His Majesty Jesus also gave his disciples authority to cast out demons. His dominion over these powers was a sign that the kingdom of God had come in His person. [Taken from *The New International Dictionary of New Testament Theology*, volume 1, pages 453–454.]

KURT E. KOCH, ThD

In a scholarly book written by a German theologian and translated into English we see the following:

Mediumistic (i.e. being a medium) abilities can either be inherited, transferred, or acquired through dabbling with the occult. These powers cannot be regarded as neutral forces of nature stemming from the subconscious, but rather the direct result of either one's own or one's ancestor's sin of sorcery. The question arises, therefore, as to what effect conversion to Christ has on these faculties.

Some Christians believe that these powers automatically disappear when a person becomes a Christian. However, in my own experience which stretches back now over 40 years, I have found that in as many as 50% of the cases have the powers of a medium that survives conversion. [Taken from *Christian Counseling and Occultism: A Complete Guidebook to Occult Oppression and Deliverance* by Kurt E. Koch, Th.D., published by Kregel Publications, 1972; page 11.]

Dr. Koch, the theologian quoted in the preceding two paragraphs, has spoken in more than a hundred seminaries and universities. His books were written and distributed a generation ago. His solution for one who has come to Christ and still has the powers of the medium "is duty-bound to ask God to remove them and replace them with the gifts of the Holy Spirit."

In my opinion, the solution would also be to cast out the occult spirits that remain. Dr. Koch's studies seem to confirm that a spirit can remain in a person after that person has become a believer in Christ.

JOHN MURRAY

The Scripture reads in Romans 12:8, "...*he who shows mercy, with cheerfulness.*" When I minister deliverance, and hopefully when I do all other kinds of ministry, I try to do ministry with cheerfulness. That does not take away from the importance of the ministry. I try not to make the person receiving ministry feel that it is an imposition for me to minister to him or her. I try to be positive and upbeat, although I take the ministry very seriously. Frankly, it is hard work.

Let's see what one scholar says about this principle of cheerful mercy:

> Oftentimes the work of mercy is disagreeable, and so it is liable to be done grudgingly and in a perfunctory way. This attitude defeats the main purpose of mercy. In Calvin's words, "For as nothing gives more solace to the sick or to any one otherwise distressed, than to see men cheerful and prompt in assisting them. To observe sadness in the countenance of those by whom assistance is given makes them to feel themselves despised." [Taken from *The Epistle to the Romans, The New International Commentary on the New Testament* by John Murray, published by Wm B. Eerdmans Publishing Co.; page 127.]

QUESTIONS TO CONSIDER

1. Which one of these quotes spoke most specifically to you and why?

2. Would you be willing to pray that more eyes, hearts, and minds be opened to the reality of the truths presented in this book?

3. Would you be willing to ask the Lord to raise up an army of people to step out in the ministry of deliverance and to walk in the authority He has given us as believers in Him?

PRAYER

Oh, most gracious heavenly Father, I humble myself before You. Please forgive me when I have doubted Your Word concerning this whole truth of spiritual warfare. I thank You for the power and authority You have given me, as a believer in Jesus, over Satan and his host. Thank You that there is glorious freedom available to me as I yield myself completely to You and command in Your authority that the enemy's chains be broken. In Jesus' most powerful name, amen.

EPILOGUE

I have written a book that comes from the passion of my heart to see individuals and families walking in freedom from spiritual bondage.

My heart cry is that the body of Christ will awaken to the reality of the spiritual battle we are in and will embrace the authority that has been given us over demonic forces even in the twenty-first century!

My hope is that this book will be of value to the curious reader, as well as to the pastor-teacher, and to the scholar.

To the curious reader I would say that I hope you will be challenged to pursue the truths presented in this book and even integrate them into your life.

To the individual who is in serious need of help, I earnestly desire that you have been instructed and that hope is arising in your heart. Seek ministry!

To the pastor-teacher, I would hope that you were encouraged both by the subject matter and by the material presented to you and that it will prove instructive in your communication and ministry in this area of spiritual warfare.

To the scholar, my hope is that this book has enough scholarly appeal that a seminary or university professor could recommend it to his or her students.

May the Lord Jesus empower and equip you as part of His victorious church!

ABOUT THE AUTHOR

Percy Burns has served as a pastor for many years in the Presbyterian Church. He received his BA from Belhaven University and his MDiv from Austin Presbyterian Seminary. He has served churches in New Orleans and Shreveport, Louisiana, and Charlotte, North Carolina. Currently he is a seminary chaplain and is on the leadership team of Charlotte Leadership Forum. He is founder of *Glorious Freedom Ministries* based in Charlotte, North Carolina.

Percy and his wife, Sara Jo, celebrated their 50th wedding anniversary in 2017, and they have four children and fourteen grandchildren.

You may visit his website at www.gloriousfreedom.org.

Experience a personal revival!

Spirit-empowered content from today's top Christian authors delivered directly to your inbox.

Join today!
lovetoreadclub.com

Inspiring Articles
Powerful Video Teaching
Resources for Revival

Get all of this and so much more, e-mailed to you twice weekly!

LOVE TO READ CLUB
by 🅳 DESTINY IMAGE